INTRODUCTION TO COMPUTERS, STRUCTURED PROGRAMMING, AND APPLICATIONS

PL/I and PL/C Language Manual

C. WILLIAM GEAR

University of Illinois
Urbana, Illinois

Library of Congress Cataloging in Publication Data

Gear, Charles William.
PL/C and PL/1 manual.

(Introduction to computers, structured programming, and applications)
Includes index.
1. PL/C (Computer program language). 2. PL/1 (Computer program language) I. Title. II. Series.
QA76.73.P23G43 001.6'424 77-18811
ISBN 0-574-21194-2

Printed in the United States of America.

10 9 8 7 6 5 4 3 2 1

PL/I AND PL/C

TABLE OF CONTENTS

PL/I AND PL/C

INTRODUCTION

This manual is a companion volume to the set of modules "Introduction to Computers, Applications, and Structured Programming." These will be referred to as the text. The text uses an informal, high-level language to describe the nature of programs that can be executed by a computer. PL/I and PL/C are high-level computer languages; languages that can be fairly readily understood by a person and yet are sufficiently precise to be processed by a computer. In practice, computers process a number of different high-level languages, including Fortran, PL/C, PL/I, Pascal, Algol, APL, Basic, Cobol, etc. Any general purpose computer installation will accept one or more of these. When first learning to program, a person should concentrate on one language, not because any one is clearly superior to others, but because minor differences between similar languages can be very confusing to the beginner (and frequently to the not so new programmer too). The following chapters will discuss PL/C and PL/I. PL/I, standing for Programming Language One, is a fairly advanced computer language, designed in the early 1960's, as a universal language that can be used for both business data processing and scientific applications. PL/C, the C standing for Cornell University, is a version of PL/I developed at Cornell University, which is particularly suitable for instructional use. PL/C includes many of the features found in PL/I, plus some additional features of particular use in program development and testing. We will describe language features found in both PL/I and PL/C in this manual. In addition, we will cover some of the special PL/C features useful to the student. To distinguish these extra features, we will use "PL/I" to refer to features found both in PL/I or PL/C, while "PL/C" will refer specifically to features found only in PL/C. We will study ways in which PL/I statements can be used to implement the ideas introduced in the text. Most of the time we will find that PL/I has statements that are simple transliterations of the informal statements used in the text, but occasionally we will find that additional statements must be used in PL/I. Although the transliteration of the program structures used in the text into PL/I may not always lead to the most straightforward way of expressing a problem in PL/I, by stressing the underlying structure of the program rather than minor details of the language, we can usually arrive at a correct code more quickly. Furthermore, we can easily convert that code into other high-level languages (as would be necessary, for example, if we wrote a large program in one language and then wished to adapt that program to another computer which did not support the first language used).

PL/I is a complex language with many capabilities, designed to be used in many different areas of application. Fortunately, it is not necessary to know about all of its capabilities to use it; the programmer does not have to know about the existence of features not used. PL/I was initially available on the IBM 360 computers. It is becoming available on other computers, but there can be minor differences between different implementations. We will discuss the form found on IBM computers.

The introductory part of this manual consists of two chapters (G1 and G2) which provide a very brief introduction to PL/I. These chapters should be read after the four chapters of the general introduction in the text have been read. This manual has chapters corresponding to each of the chapters in Module P of the text. Each should be read after the corresponding chapter in the text. As language features are introduced in Module P, their specific forms in PL/I are discussed in this manual. Some of the applications and algorithms in Module A of the text are covered in the chapters of Part A of this manual, which gives PL/I versions of the programs developed in the text. Part C of this manual is a reference section, providing a summary of language and features of common PL/I and PL/C implementations. This volume is designed to be read in conjunction with the text; it is not intended as a separate primer on PL/I, because the general principles of programming languages are described in the text, and are not duplicated here. The information in this volume indicates the particular manner in which these general language principles are implemented in PL/I, and the ways in which PL/I differs from these general principles.

The numbering of chapters in Parts P and A of this volume corresponds exactly to the numbering in the text. Thus Chapter P1 of this volume discusses numeric data types in PL/I while chapter P1 in the text discusses the general principles behind different types of numeric data. Because references are made both to the main text and to other chapters in this manual, they are distinguished by underlining. References to this manual are underlined. Thus Chapter P1 refers to a chapter in this manual, while Chapter P1 refers to the text. Programs from Modules P and A that appear in this manual have corresponding numbers. Thus, Program P2.1 in this manual corresponds to Program P2.1 in Chapter P2 of the text.

Problems concerning aspects of PL/I appear at the end of chapters in Parts P and A of this manual. In addition, there is a list at the end of each chapter of programs in the text that can be converted to PL/I as exercises in transliterating programs from the pseudo language to PL/I, and an indication of problems in the main text which can also be answered in PL/I.

G1 USING A COMPUTER IN PL/I and PL/C

Let us start with a trivial example of a PL/I program. Program G1.1 executes the steps of one of those children's number games in which a child is asked to "Think of a number, add ten to it, double it, subtract six from it, halve it, take away the number first thought of, and, surprise, surprise, the answer is that magic number seven."

Program G1.1 Children's Game

```
GAME: PROCEDURE OPTIONS(MAIN);

    /* PROGRAM TO EXECUTE THE STEPS IN THE CHILD'S GAME: */
    /*   "THINK OF A NUMBER. ADD 10 TO IT, DOUBLE IT,    */
    /*    SUBTRACT 6, HALVE IT, AND SUBTRACT THE NUMBER  */
    /*    YOU FIRST THOUGHT OF."                         */

    DECLARE (I, J, K, L, M, N) FIXED DECIMAL;

        GET LIST (I); /* INPUT THE "NUMBER THOUGHT OF" */
        J = I + 10;
        K = J + J;
        L = K - 6;
        M = L/2;
        N = M - I;
        PUT LIST ('YOUR INPUT WAS',I,'THE RESULT IS',N);
    END GAME;
```

The program consists of a number of lines. The first line gives the name of the program, GAME. In PL/I, programs are called procedures. The meaning of the rest of the line, OPTIONS(MAIN), should be ignored at this time. All of our programs will start in this way; we will discuss its meaning later. The next four non-blank lines are comments. Comments appear between the character pairs /* and */, the former preceding the comment and the latter terminating it. Comments can include any text except the combination */ which terminates the comment. Comments may appear almost anywhere in PL/I. For example, a comment appears following a later statement in this program. The next line is blank. Blank lines may appear anywhere in PL/I, and are useful for separating pieces of the program visually. The next line declares the variables I, J, K, L, M, and N to be FIXED DECIMAL. This tells the compiler information about the type of data to be used. In this case, it says that the variables I, J, K, L, M, and N will hold the familiar decimal numbers such as -15, 373, etc. We will delay further discussion of declarations until Chapter P1.

The first statement in this program that causes any action is the GET LIST (I) statement which tells the computer to get a value for the variable I from the input device. GET LIST (...); is the equivalent of input ... in our informal language. When this statement is executed, the computer reads a number from the input device, and makes the value of the variable I equal to the value of the number read.

The next five statements of the program assign values to J, K, L, M, and N in turn. Each is executed before its successor. For example, J = I + 10; forms the value of I + 10 and makes the value of J equal to this. The value of I used to form I + 10 is the value set in I by the previous GET LIST statement. The next statement in the program is an output statement, PUT LIST (...);. It functions the same as the output ... statement in our informal language. A list of items to be output can appear inside the parentheses in the PUT LIST statement. In this case, we have included some character strings, such as 'YOUR INPUT WAS', and some variables, such as I and N. The character strings are printed directly, while the value of the variables are printed. For example, if I has the value 34, and N has the value 7, this statement prints the line

```
    YOUR INPUT WAS           34       THE RESULT IS            7
```

on the output device. The last statement in the program is an END statement, indicating the physical end of the procedure.

Note that all statements are followed by a semi-colon. The semi-colon indicates the end of a statement. In PL/I, statements may run over several lines if desired, or several statements may be placed on one line. For example, we could have placed three statements on a single line by writing

```
J = I + 10; K = J + J; L = K - 6;
```

However, in general it is preferable to start each statement on a separate line for ease of reading.

Blanks may appear almost anywhere in PL/I. We have used them to separate operators such as + and = from variables and numbers. We have also used them to indent the lines of the program to give it a clean appearance. Blanks may not appear in the middle of names or keywords, but they must appear between adjacent names and keywords. Thus, we cannot write GET LIST as GETLIST, GAME as GA ME, or DECLARE as DEC LARE. Otherwise, the only time that a blank is significant is in a character string. Thus, the blanks in 'YOUR INPUT WAS' are needed to separate the words in the output. Comments may appear anywhere that blanks can appear except inside character strings. Comments may run across several lines. For example, it was not necessary to surround each of the four lines of comment in Program G1.1 by the /* and */ pairs. The four lines could have been treated as one comment by starting the first line with /* and ending the fourth line with */. PL/C has an option which allows the user to restrict comments to a single line. It is a good idea to use this, as a common error is to forget to terminate a comment with */, causing all subsequent lines to be taken as part of the comment until the end of the next comment. This error can also arise when the terminating */ is placed beyond column 72, so that it is ignored by the compiler. (Most PL/C compilers restrict comments to a single line unless the user specifies otherwise. Chapter C4 indicates how this is done.) Thus, the four lines of comments in Program G1.1 are each surrounded by the comment enclosing /* and */ pairs.

Each PL/I statement tells the compiler about the program or about about some action that is to be taken. In the example above, the assignment statements such as "J = I + 10;", the input statement GET LIST, and the output statement PUT LIST are executable statements that indicate an action to be performed. The DECLARE and END are non-executable statements that tell the computer about the program. The last statement in any PL/I program must be an END statement.

Once a program is written in PL/I, or any other language, it must be communicated to the computer. There are a number of ways of doing this, including punched cards and computer terminals. Some of these are discussed in Chapters G1 and C4. As far as PL/I is concerned, there is no essential difference between the various ways of communicating with the computer. A PL/I program consists of a number of lines of characters, a line being either the set of characters on a single card or the set of characters typed on a single line from a terminal. We will discuss punched cards, but everything is applicable to terminal-oriented systems. Before Program G1.1 can be executed, it must be punched on cards and submitted to the computer. On most computer systems, the PL/I program must be punched in columns 2 through 72 only. Column 1 should be left blank, and columns 73 through 80 can be used for any purpose. Columns 73 to 80 of punched cards are often used for identification. They are ignored by the PL/I compiler. A common identification system is to punch a four letter abbreviation of the name of the program in columns 73 to 76 and to punch a four digit sequence number in columns 77 to 80.

When a program is submitted to a computer system, it is necessary to tell the computer which language was used to write the program because most computers accept several languages. This aspect of computer usage is very implementation dependent. Program G1.1a shows the lines of information that must be submitted for a PL/C job on a typical IBM 360/370 installation. (All complete programs in this manual have been run under PL/C. If you have a choice, this is the best for checking your programs. If you are using PL/I on IBM computers and do not have access to PL/C, you have a choice of a checkout compiler, or an optimizing compiler. The former should be used while testing programs, as it gives more diagnostic information about errors than the optimizing compiler which concentrates on efficient execution of your program.) We see that the lines of Program G1.1 have been preceded and followed by a number of additional lines. These lines contain system control information which give information to the computer system. In this example, the first four lines tell the computer the identity of the user and that a PL/C job is to be processed. The next line, $PL/C, tells the PL/C compiler that a PL/C program appears on the following cards. (On many systems, the character * is used in place of the $, so the first line would be *PLC.) Subsequent cards are translated by the PL/C compiler into internal form. The next line starting with a $ character, $DATA, tells the PL/C compiler that subsequent lines contain data to be processed by the executing program. This terminates processing by the PL/C compiler, and the user program begins execution. The data for the run, in this case one line containing the number 34, appears after the $DATA card. The system control information that must appear before and after your program may be different at your computer installation, so your instructor or computer center will tell you what items of information must appear.

Program G1.1a Childrens' Game

```
//PLCPROGR JOB
/*ID PS=3503
/*ID NAME=GEAR
//  EXEC PLC
$PL/C
    GAME: PROCEDURE OPTIONS(MAIN);

        /* PROGRAM TO EXECUTE THE STEPS IN THE CHILD'S GAME: */
        /*  "THINK OF A NUMBER. ADD 10 TO IT, DOUBLE IT,     */
        /*    SUBTRACT 6, HALVE IT, AND SUBTRACT THE NUMBER  */
        /*    YOU FIRST THOUGHT OF."                         */

        DECLARE (I, J, K, L, M, N) FIXED DECIMAL;

            GET LIST (I); /* READ THE "NUMBER THOUGHT OF" */
            J = I + 10;
            K = J + J;
            L = K - 6;
            M = L/2;
            N = M - I;
            PUT LIST ('YOUR INPUT WAS',I,'THE RESULT IS',N);
        END GAME;
$DATA
34
/*
```

The output generated by the computer when Program G1.1a is run is shown in Figure G1.1. The output is shown approximately as it was printed by the computer. (Some of the lines have been shortened and some irrelevant information has been removed.) We notice that the source deck is reproduced (which is handy for checking errors). Immediately following the END statement is a diagnostic message called a warning. This is an indication of a possible error. In this case the "error" is the fact that "NO FILE SPECIFIED. SYSIN/SYSPRINT ASSUMED." This means that the programmer has not specified from where the input for the GET LIST statement is to be obtained, or to where the output from the PUT LIST statement is to be sent. Consequently, the compiler has assumed SYSIN and SYSPRINT, which are the names of the standard input device and the standard output device, that is, the card reader and printer in a card-oriented system, or the terminal in a terminal system.

Since there were no errors, only warnings, the program was executed. The result of the execution is to read the data following the $DATA card shown in Program G1.1a. The value 34 is assigned to the variable I, and, after execution of the intervening assignment statements, the PUT LIST statement prints the answer shown. At this time, the variables I and N have the values 34 and 7 respectively. After termination of the program we are told where the program stopped, the values of the variables when the program terminates (called a DUMP), and some statistics about our use of the computer - including how much time was used. Notice that two sets of statistics are listed, one called compilation statistics and one called execution statistics. Compilation of the PL/C program to internal form took 27/100 of a second. Execution of the internal form took 2/100 of a second.

```
//PLCPROGR JOB (3503),TIME=(0000,10),MSGLEVEL=(2,0)          JOB 135
//*ID PS=(3503,1087)
//*ID NAME=GEAR
//*ID SYSTEM=EXPRESS
//  EXEC PLC
$PL/C

 GAME: PROCEDURE OPTIONS(MAIN);
  STMT LEVEL   SOURCE TEXT
     1       GAME: PROCEDURE OPTIONS(MAIN);

               /* PROGRAM TO EXECUTE THE STEPS IN THE CHILD'S GAME: */
               /*   "THINK OF A NUMBER. ADD 10 TO IT, DOUBLE IT,    */
               /*    SUBTRACT 6, HALVE IT, AND SUBTRACT THE NUMBER  */
               /*    YOU FIRST THOUGHT OF."                         */

     2    1       DECLARE (I, J, K, L, M, N) FIXED DECIMAL;

     3    1         GET LIST (I); /* READ THE "NUMBER THOUGHT OF" */
     4    1         J = I + 10;
     5    1         K = J + J;
     6    1         L = K - 6;
     7    1         M = L/2;
     8    1         N = M - I;
     9    1         PUT LIST ('YOUR INPUT WAS',I,'THE RESULT IS',N);
    10    1       END GAME;
ERRORS/WARNINGS DETECTED DURING CODE GENERATION:
      WARNING: NO FILE SPECIFIED. SYSIN/SYSPRINT ASSUMED. (CG0C)

YOUR INPUT WAS             34                THE RESULT IS              7

IN STMT   10  PROGRAM RETURNS FROM MAIN PROCEDURE.
PL/C-R7   POST-MORTEM DUMP   PAGE   1

***** MAIN PROCEDURE GAME

N=        7              M=       41              L=       82
K=       88              J=       44              I=       34

        COMPILATION STATISTICS  (0010 STATEMENTS)
SECONDS  ERRORS  WARNINGS  PAGES  LINES  CARDS  INCL'S
    .27       0         1      1     33     18       0
                 EXECUTION STATISTICS
SECONDS  ERRORS  WARNINGS  PAGES  LINES  CARDS  INCL'S  AUX I/O
    .02       0         0      1      5      1       0        0
```

Fig. G1.1 Output Generated by Prog. G1.1a

G2 CODING A PROGRAM IN PL/I

In this chapter we will take a brief look at some PL/I statements. However, details of these and other statements will be left for later chapters. Our purpose here is to see that we can take a program in an informal high-level language such as the one used in the text, and code it in PL/I. The conversion is basically a transliteration, that is, a simple replacement of words and characters in the first language by words and characters in the second language, using simple rules.

Let us start with Program G2.1a to compute tax. It consists of a mixture of statements, some of which use keywords such as do forever, and some of which use variables and constants. The variables have names, and we can use the same names in PL/I provided that they satisfy the PL/I naming rules. In this manual, we will restrict ourselves to the following forms of PL/I names: they will start with a letter, and can be followed by zero to thirty characters, each of which can be a letter, decimal digit, or underline character. (PL/I actually allows three additional characters to be used, but we will not use them.) Note that a blank cannot be part of a name. Every one of the variable names in the text satisfy this form, so we will be able to use the same names.

We have also given names to the programs. In the text these names have the same form as variable names. Most of the time this is also true in PL/I, but there are situations in which the name of a program (GAME in Program G1.1, and COMPTAX in Program G2.1) must be much shorter -- a maximum of seven characters on many systems. Therefore, we will abbreviate program names to a maximum of seven characters.

Some of the statements in Program G2.1a can be written directly, for example

```
TAXABLE_INCOME = INCOME - DEDUCTIONS - 750.0*DEPENDENTS;
```

This is similar to the corresponding statement in Program G2.1a except that the left arrow has been replaced by the = character. The action however, is still one of assignment. The value of the expression following the = is assigned to the variable named TAXABLE_INCOME. Thereafter, TAXABLE_INCOME has that value until changed by another statement. The statement uses the constant 750.0. Usually, constants can be written in the natural way. We will cover rules for writing constants in Chapter P1. One of the assignment statements uses the function MAX which computes the maximum of several items. This can be used directly in PL/I. The keyword input is replaced in PL/I by "GET LIST(...)" to get the input statement

```
GET LIST (INCOME, DEPENDENTS, EXPENSES);
```

We will be covering the GET LIST statement in detail in Chapter P6.

The first GET LIST statement above reads three numbers. They must be punched on one or more cards (lines) following the program. Each number must be separated from the next by a comma and/or one or more blanks. For example, if this GET LIST statement reads a line containing "10000   3, 850", it will assign the values 10000, 3, and 850 to the variables INCOME, DEPENDENTS, and EXPENSES. (Note that 10000 cannot be punched as 10,000.)

The keyword output is replaced by PUT LIST (...), to get the output statement

```
PUT LIST (TAX)
```

We can also output character strings by enclosing them in quotes as shown in Program G2.1.

G2 CODING A PROGRAM IN PL/I

The keywords _program_ and _endprogram_ are replaced by PROCEDURE OPTIONS(MAIN) and END respectively. This leaves the keyword groups _do forever_ ... _enddo_ and _if_ ... _then_ ... _else_ ... _endif_. The former group will be written as

```
DO WHILE ('1'B);
   statements inside loop
   END;
```

DO WHILE ('1'B) means the same as _do forever_. (Formally, it says "do the loop while the condition '1'B is true. Later we will see that '1'B is the PL/I way of indicating something that is always true.) The latter group uses the PL/I IF-THEN-ELSE structure. For example, the informal language code

```
if A > B
  then C <- D
  else E <- F
  endif
```

will be translated into the PL/I

```
IF A > B
   THEN C = D;
   ELSE E = F;
```

The PL/I IF statement is very similar to the _if_ statement used informally in the text, but it _does not_ have an _endif_ keyword to indicate the end of the _if_ group. Instead, the keywords THEN and ELSE can only be followed by a single section of code such as a statement. Until we discuss IF statements in detail in Chapter _P3_, we will restrict ourselves to simple IF statements of the above form. Note that we use indentation in both DO loops and IF statements to make them more readable.

Using these rules, Program G2.1a can be translated into PL/I as shown in Program _G2.1_. Note that we have used comments within the DECLARE statement, and it spread over several lines. These comments indicate the use of those variables whose names may not be completely obvious. These comments appear where blanks can appear.

The first statement following the PROCEDURE statement in Program _G2.1_ is a declaration of the variables. Declarations are covered in Chapter _P1_, where we will see that the declaration FLOAT DECIMAL allows the variables to take on decimal values such as 13253.24, representing 13253 dollars and 24 cents.

The program can be punched as shown, but some flexibility is allowed. We will use blanks around many of the operators, and also use indentation so that each program structure, such as a DO ... END, extends from the first statement to immediately before the next line at the same level of indentation. For example, the IF statement in Program _G2.1_ extends to just before the TAX = MAX(TAX,0.0) statement.

This program can be executed by surrounding it with the appropriate system control cards -- those starting with / and $ in Program _1.1a_.

Example -- Finding the Largest Number

Program G2.2a uses a simple loop to find the largest of a set of 20 input values. That program introduces the _do while_ statement. We can translate this statement almost directly into PL/I. The set of statements

G2 CODING A PROGRAM IN PL/I

Program G2.1 Income Tax Computation

```
COMPTAX: PROCEDURE OPTIONS(MAIN);
    /* INDIVIDUAL INCOME TAX IS CALCULATED.                    */
    /*   FIRST THE MAXIMUM DEDUCTION IS CALCULATED,            */
    /*   THEN THE TAXABLE INCOME IS FOUND.                     */
    /*   FINALLY THE TAX IS CALCULATED USING ONE               */
    /*   OF TWO RATES, DEPENDING ON THE INCOME.                */
    /*   IF THE RESULT IS NEGATIVE, THE TAX IS SET TO 0.       */

    DECLARE   (INCOME,        /*       ANNUAL INCOME - INPUT */
            DEPENDENTS,   /*     # OF DEPENDENTS - INPUT    */
            EXPENSES,     /* DEDUCTIBLE EXPENSES - INPUT    */
            DEDUCTIONS,   /*         TOTAL TAX DEDUCTIONS   */
            TAXABLE_INCOME,
            TAX)          FLOAT DECIMAL;

        DO WHILE ('1'B);
            GET LIST (INCOME, DEPENDENTS, EXPENSES);
            DEDUCTIONS = MAX(EXPENSES, 0.15*INCOME);
            TAXABLE_INCOME = INCOME - DEDUCTIONS - 750.0*DEPENDENTS;
            IF TAXABLE_INCOME < 4000
                THEN TAX = 0.15*TAXABLE_INCOME;
                ELSE TAX = 600.0 + 0.2*(TAXABLE_INCOME - 4000.0);
            TAX = MAX(TAX, 0.0);
            PUT LIST ('TAX IS', TAX);
            END;
    END COMPTAX;
```

Program G2.2 Largest of a Set of Numbers

```
FNDLARG: PROCEDURE OPTIONS(MAIN);

    /* PROGRAM TO READ 20 VALUES AND OUTPUT THE LARGEST */

    DECLARE (LARGE,     /* LARGEST VALUE READ SO FAR     */
        NUMBER,    /* NEXT INPUT VALUE              */
        COUNT)     /* NUMBER OF VALUES READ SO FAR */
          FIXED DECIMAL;

        GET LIST (LARGE);
        COUNT = 1;
        DO WHILE (COUNT < 20);
            GET LIST (NUMBER);
            IF NUMBER > LARGE
                THEN LARGE = NUMBER;
                ELSE ;
            COUNT = COUNT + 1;
            END;
        PUT LIST ('LARGEST VALUE IS', LARGE);
    END FNDLARG;
```

```
    do while condition
      statement list
      enddo
```

will be translated into the PL/I code

```
DO WHILE (condition)
   statement list
   END
```

Problems

1. Find out how to use your computer for PL/I programs, and punch and run Program G2.1. Run several sets of data.

2. Modify Program G2.1 so that it also allows for medical expenses MEDICAL to be deducted in they exceed 3% of INCOME and if EXPENSES rather than 15% of INCOME is used as the deduction.

3. Modify Program G2.2 so that it finds the minimum of 25 numbers.

P1 DATA

Every constant or variable used in a PL/I program has a data type. PL/I has a very rich class of data types. In this chapter we will discuss two types of PL/I numeric data corresponding to reals and integers. Other types of numeric and non-numeric data will be covered in Chapter P9.

PL/I variable names were defined in Chapter 2 to consist of 31 or fewer alphanumeric characters. In general, PL/I systems allow only upper case-letters, since the lower-case letters are not available on most key punches used with PL/I. PL/C does not allow the keywords such as DO, IF, etc, to be used as names, so the PL/C user must avoid the list of keywords given in Chapter C1. Blanks may not appear within names, nor may a name cross a card boundary. Although PL/I does not require that the data type of all variables be declared explicitly, we will make declarations of every variable used. This is done with the non-executable DECLARE statement. For example,

```
DECLARE   (C24, RABID, INT1)   FIXED DECIMAL;
```

declares the three variables named in the parentheses to be fixed-point numbers represented decimally. With this declaration, the point is at the right end of the numbers, with five digits of precision (in IBM PL/I compilers). Hence the range of these numbers is -99999 to +99999, and they are integers.

Each variable is allocated a cell in memory to hold its value, as described in Chapter G4. Most computers can also represent numbers in binary format, as described in Chapter C1. PL/I allows the programmer to specify binary representation by replacing DECIMAL with BINARY in the declaration. For example,

```
DECLARE   (J, N)   FIXED BINARY;
```

specifies that the values of the variables J and N are represented in binary internally. In that case, they have a range of -32767 to +32767 in the IBM PL/I compilers. Fortunately, the user does not have to be concerned with the internal form of storage while programming. It is recommended that beginning programmers declare all numeric variables to be decimally represented. BINARY representation is only recommended in large programs that do a lot of computation; in that case we get improved efficiency with BINARY.

Variables with real values are declared to be of type FLOAT. For example,

```
DECLARE   (A, B, Z, X2)  FLOAT DECIMAL
```

declares the four variables named to be represented in floating point. On IBM PL/I compilers they have about seven digits of precision and and an exponent range from about -78 to +75. (We say "about" because the compiler "cheats" and represents everything internally in binary in the IBM PL/I compilers.) The declaration

```
DECLARE   (A, B, Z, X2)  FLOAT BINARY;
```

has the same effect. As with fixed-point numbers, each variable is allocated a cell in memory to hold its value.

If any variable is not declared, PL/I assumes that a variable starting with the letters I, J, K, L, M, or N is an integer and that the rest are reals. Although it seems that the use of these <u>default</u> declarations can save time, it is easy to make an error by using a name such as LOW for a real value and forget that it is assumed to be an integer by the compiler. Hence, it is recommended that you declare every variable.

You can declare as many variables as you like in a single declaration statement. The statement can spread over several lines. If a declaration statement contains just one variable, the parentheses are not necessary. For example,

```
DECLARE  Y  FLOAT DECIMAL;
```

Groups of variables of different types can be declared in a single declaration statement. The keywords DECLARE, DECIMAL, and BINARY can be abbreviated to DCL, DEC, and BIN respectively. For example,

```
DCL (C24, RABID, INT1)   FIXED DEC,
    (A, B, Z, X1)        FLOAT BIN;
```

is equivalent to

```
DECLARE (C24, RABID, INIT1) FIXED DECIMAL;
DECLARE (A, B, Z, X2)       FLOAT BINARY;
```

Note that a comma follows the first part of the declaration in the first example rather than a semi-colon; this tells the compiler that the declaration is continued. No variable may appear in more than one declaration statement in the same part of the program. Clearly it makes no sense to declare a variable to be both FIXED and FLOAT! Declarations tell the compiler how variables are to be stored and used in arithmetic.

Program P1.1 is a PL/I version of Program P1.1. A negative value of VALUE is used to indicate the end of the input. All of the variables are stored in floating point except for N. The GET LIST and PUT LIST statements know which form of data to use because they can tell the type from the declaration statements. Similarly PL/I can tell from the the variable declarations what form of arithmetic to use. In this example, the division of the floating-point value TOTAL by the fixed-point value N yields a floating-point result. Later we will learn what happens when more than one type of data is used in an arithmetic expression.

Program P1.1 Average of a Set of Positive Input Values

```
AVERAGE: PROCEDURE OPTIONS (MAIN);

    /*  PROGRAM FOR AVERAGE OF A SET OF POSITIVE INPUT NUMBERS */
    /*  END OF FILE IS INDICATED BY NEGATIVE NUMBER            */

    DECLARE  (AVERAGE, TOTAL, VALUE) FLOAT DECIMAL,
              N                      FIXED DECIMAL;

            N = 0;
        TOTAL = 0.0E0;
        GET LIST (VALUE);
        DO WHILE (VALUE >= 0.0E0);
            N = N + 1;
            TOTAL = TOTAL + VALUE;
            GET LIST (VALUE);
            END;
        AVERAGE = TOTAL/N;
        PUT LIST ( 'AVERAGE OF',N,'VALUES IS',AVERAGE);
    END AVERAGE;
```

P1 DATA

PL/I can tell the difference between integer and floating-point constants by the way they are punched. The rules are slightly different to those given in Chapter P1. Floating-point constants must have an exponent. An exponent is specified as the character E followed by a signed or unsigned integer. If there is no exponent, a numeric constant is represented internally in fixed-point form. If there is no point or it is at the right hand end of a constant with no exponent, the internal form is an integer. Consequently, we will always type PL/I integers without a decimal point, while we will always use an exponent <u>and</u> a decimal point in a floating-point constant. Thus, 1, 15, and -36 are our ways of entering integer constants, while 45.3E-5, -34.2E3, and 1.0E0 are our ways of entering floating-point constants. (We will not write constants of the form 5.63, that is, with an embedded point and no exponent for now, as these are represented internally in <u>fixed point</u>, a data type to be discussed in Chapter <u>P9</u>.) Blanks may not appear between the characters of an constant, a constant may not cross a card boundary, nor may other punctuation be used. For example, 12 452 and 12,452 are invalid ways of punching 12452.

<u>Problems</u>

1. Write the following constants in their PL/I forms:

   (a) 2 x 10 (b) 3 1/4 (c) 2,163 (d) 3.5 million (integer)
   (e) 2,000 (floating point) (f) 1/3 (g) .0000000001

2. Which of the following are valid PL/I names?

   (a) WEST (b) S3.2 (c) LONG-SHOT (d) LONGSHOT
   (e) EAST30 (f) 30EAST (g) SHORT (h) small
   (i) EAST_30 (j) _LAST

P2 ASSIGNMENT STATEMENTS AND ARITHMETIC

An assignment statement in PL/I has the form

```
SUM = SUM + X*Y;
```

The expression on the right hand side is evaluated and assigned to the variable on the left hand side. At this point, the values of the right hand and left hand sides are equal, but assignment by later statements of values to any of the variables involved can change that. Therefore, the PL/I programmer must learn to interpret the character = as an operation implying assignment, not as a statement of equality. Rules for PL/I assignment statements are almost identical to the rules given in Chapter P2. The precedence rules for operators in Table P2.1 apply to PL/I with the exceptions noted below. Hence, exponentiation (represented in PL/I by **) is performed before multiplication (*) and division (/), which in turn are performed before addition (+) and subtraction (-). Within operators of the same precedence level, evaluation proceeds from left to right except as noted for exponentiation and unary operators in special rules 2 an 3 below. Parentheses can be used to override the built-in precedence rules.

Special PL/I Rules for Operators and Precedence

1. There is only one division operator, represented by /. It has the precedence given in Table P2.1. Its effect when at least one of its operands is floating point is as given in the text. It is better to avoid its use on fixed-point operands because the result is difficult to describe at this stage.

2. Exponentiation is represented by **. Thus A**B means A to the power B.

3. Unary plus and minus have the same precedence level as exponentiation. However, although the left-to-right rule is followed for all other operators of the same precedence, exponentiation and the unary operators obey a right-to-left rule. Thus, A**-B is the same as A**(-B), while A**B**C is the same as A**(B**C). Because these rules differ from language to language, it is better to use parenthesization to avoid any ambiguity for the reader.

Examples

The expressions in the examples at the start of Section P2.2 can be written as

```
(i)      (A + 5*B)/(16.4 + C)

(ii)     (X**2 + Y**2)**0.5

(iii)    (-B + SQRT(B**2 -4*A*C)/(2*A)
```

The distance between a pair of points with coordinates (X1, Y1) and (X2, Y2) can be calculated by the assignment statement

```
DISTANCE = ((X2 - X1)**2 + (Y2 - Y1)**2)**0.5;
```

Chapter P2 also gives rules for determining the data type that results when an operation uses two different types of operands. These rules apply to mixed operands PL/I with the exceptions in noted in the list below. Also, the rules for rounding and truncation are those in Chapter P2 with the exceptions noted below.

Special PL/I Rules for Mixed Data Types

1. If an fixed-point valued expression is assigned to a real variable, for example in the statement A = 12345678, truncation rather than rounding takes place when the length of the fixed-point value is greater than the precision that can be represented in floating point. However, in the cases presented so far, the precision of floating-point value is about seven decimal digits, more than are represented in either DECIMAL or BINARY fixed-point values. Therefore, in these cases the conversion introduces no errors.

2. If a floating-point value is converted to a fixed-point value and there is insufficient space for the digits, truncation occurs.

3. The divide operation is always represented by /. If one or both operands are floating-point values, the result is a floating-point value, so that 3.0E0/2 is 1.5E0, but if both operands are fixed-point values, the result is determined by some complex PL/I rules which will not be covered in detail in this manual. Usually, the result is what is wanted, namely a reasonably close approximation to the quotient, but the rules used can lead to some apparently strange results -- results which signal overflow conditions, so that no errors occur without warning, but ones which are a nuisance to deal with. In general, it is better to avoid division of fixed-point values. (Some additional information is given in the Chapter P9 under the discussion of fixed-point data types.)

4. If a fixed-point value X is raised to a power that is other than a non-negative integer constant, X is converted to floating-point, so that the result is a floating-point number. Thus, 45**(-3) has a floating-point value, whereas 45**3 has a fixed-point value. 45**I has a floating-point value even if I is an fixed-point variable containing the positive integer 3.

5. Conversion between DECIMAL and BINARY can cause truncation because the range of fixed-point values may be different.

When a constant such as one-third is needed, it can be computed by writing 1.0E0/3.0E0 but this means that it will be computed each time that it is used. This can be avoided by assigning the value to a variable at the start of the program by writing, for example, "ONE_THIRD =1.0E0/3.0E0" and using the variable ONE_THIRD whenever one third is needed. Alternatively, the constant 0.3333333E0 can be used, but this may not define the value to the full precision of the computer.

The beginning programmer should be particularly careful with the division operation because it is easy to write an expression such as (A**2 + B**2)**(1/3) when the one-third power of A**2 + B**2 is wanted, instead of (A**2 + B**2)**(1.0E0/3.0E0). Whenever a division is written, be certain that at least one of its operands is a floating-point value or that you know the action of the division operation in the particular case.

Because there is no integer division operation, one of the PL/I built-in functions described in part C must be used. For example, TRUNC(X) yields a value equal to the integer part of X. Thus, TRUNC(3.6E0) is 3.0E0, while TRUNC(-4.8E0) is 4.0E0. The integer part of a quotient can be found by writing TRUNC(A/B). It is better to make at least one of A and B real in this expression so that the division in done in floating point. If A and B are both fixed point, the function FLOAT can be used to convert one of them by writing TRUNC(FLOAT(A)/B).

Because PL/I automatically converts data types when mixed mode arithmetic is performed, we can write expressions such as A + 1, where A is a floating-point variable. However, we will write constants in the correct form. That is, we will write A + 3.0E0 rather than A + 3, because the former leads to more efficient programs--the PL/I compiler does not have to make the conversion from fixed point to floating point for us. The correct form of constants is used in Program P2.1, which is a PL/I version of Program P2.1.

Program P2.1 Compute Fill for Road Contractor

```
COMPFIL: PROCEDURE OPTIONS(MAIN);

    /*  PROGRAM TO COMPUTE FILL AND TRUCK USAGE                  */
    /*   THE INPUT DATA MUST CONSIST OF                          */
    /*     FIRST CARD:  W, T                                     */
    /*           WHERE W IF THE AMOUNT OF FILL NEEDED TO         */
    /*           FILL 100 METERS OF ROAD UP 1 METER, AND         */
    /*         T IS THE AMOUNT OF FILL CARRIED BY A TRUCK.       */
    /*     SECOND AND SUBSEQUENT CARDS:                          */
    /*      H, THE HEIGHT OF CONSECUTIVE                         */
    /*      100 METER SECTIONS OF THE PROPOSED ROAD.             */
    /*     LAST CARD:    ANY NEGATIVE VALUE.                     */

    /* OUTPUT IS AMOUNT OF FILL AND NUMBER OF TRUCK-METERS       */
    /*     NEEDED FOR JOB.                                       */

    DECLARE  (D,            /* DISTANCE ALONG ROAD    */
            FILL,           /* AMOUNT OF FILL NEEDED  */
            HAUL,           /* NUMBER OF TRUCK-METERS */
            W, T, H)  FLOAT DECIMAL;
        FILL = 0.0E0;
        HAUL = 0.0E0;
        D = 0.0E0;
        GET LIST (W, T);
        GET LIST (H);
        DO WHILE (H >= 0.0E0);
            D = D + 100.0E0;
            FILL = FILL + H;
            HAUL = HAUL + H*D;
            GET LIST (H);
            END;
        FILL = FILL*W;
        HAUL = 2.0E0*HAUL*W/T;
        PUT LIST ('FILL IS',FILL,'TRUCK-METERS ARE',HAUL);
    END COMPFIL;
```

In PL/I, the built-in arithmetic functions such as ABS, MAX, MIN, etc., return a result with the same data type as their argument(s). In the case of functions with multiple arguments, arguments are converted as necessary so that all have the same type. Thus, MAX(3, 2.7E0, 4) is 4.0E0 because the fixed-point arguments 3 and 4 are first converted to floating point. The mathematical functions such as SQRT and SIN all operate on floating-point arguments; if the argument supplied by the programmer is fixed point, it is automatically converted to floating point. Thus SQRT(4) and SQRT(4.E0) both yield the result 2.0E0. This topic is covered in detail in Chapter P7, and the PL/I and PL/C built-in arithmetic functions are listed in Chapter C3.

P2 ASSIGNMENT STATEMENTS AND ARITHMETIC

Problems

1. What is the value of each of the following expressions in PL/I?

    a. 34.5E0*2 + 1
    b. -17/2E0 + 9
    c. -15*4 + 4.
    d. TRUNC(35./(-6.0E0))
    e. (232 - 22.)*(2.5E0 - 1.5E0)

2. What values are left in each of the variables used in the following code?

```
DECLARE (A, B, C, D) FLOAT DECIMAL,
        (I, J, K, L) FIXED DECIMAL;
A = 3.5E1;
B = 27;
I = A - 1.2E0;
J = -3.6E0;
C = 3.0E0*A - I;
K = C/I;
D = SQRT(-3.*J);
L = TRUNC((I - J)/FLOAT(K)) + A/B;
```

3. Write PL/I expressions for

    a. The B-th real power of real variable A.
    b. The integer part of real A divided by real B.

4. If the first day of the month is a Tuesday, and the current date in the month is N (a fixed-point value), write a PL/I expression whoes value is a fixed-point integer with a value between 1 and 7 corresponding to to the current day of the week. The value 1 should represent Monday, 2 Tuesday, etc. Thus, if N contains 23, the value of the expression should be 3. (You will need to use the PL/I function FIXED to get a fixed-point result.)

5. Write a program to read an integer greater than 2 and to determine if it is prime. (An integer N is prime if it is not divisible by any integer between 2 and N-1 inclusive.)

6. Write a program to print all integers between 1 and 100 that are perfect squares.

7. Write a program to print all integers between 1 and 50 that are not perfect squares.

Problem in text to do in PL/I: 3.

P3 CONTROL

The principle control structures in a program are the *do-enddo* and *if-then-else* structures. PL/I has forms for these structures that are very close to the forms used in our informal language. These forms use the same keywords except that *enddo* is replaced with END, the same keyword used to end a program. The IF statement tests a condition, and the continued execution of a loop is determined by the testing of a similar condition. In PL/I, conditions are tested much as in Chapter P3, by comparing a pair of values with one of the six relational operators. Thus, "A < 0.0E0" is *true* if the value of A is negative; it is *false* if the value of A is zero or positive. The six conditional operators are shown in Table P3.1. Note that when the keypunch does not have a single character corresponding to the usual mathematical symbol for the operation, such as ≠ for not equal, two characters are used. These two characters follow the order in which we usually speak the operation, such as >= for "greater than or equal."

Table P3.1 PL/I Comparison Operators

operator	meaning	opposite condition
<	Less than	>=
>	Greater than	<=
<=	Less than or equal	>
>=	Greater than or equal	<
=	Equal	¬=
¬=	Not equal	=

Examples

```
1.3E0  > 1.2E0           is true
6.5E1 <= 13/2.0E-1       is true
4 - 2 ¬= 2               is false
```

The forms in which the basic structures are written in PL/I are discussed in the next two sections.

P3.1 Loops

The PL/I transliteration of

```
do-while condition
  body of loop
  enddo
```

is

```
DO WHILE (condition);
   body of loop
   END;
```

Note that the only significant changes are the parentheses around the condition--these must be present--and the use of END for *enddo*. As noted earlier, each statement is terminated with a semi-colon. The indentation is important for the human reader--it gives a visual clue to the extent of the loop--but it is irrelevant to the compiler. As the code below illustrates, the body of the loop is indented to the right of the DO; after the loop ends, the next line starts in the same column as the DO. The code below prints the amount remaining on a mortgage of C dollars at an annual interest rate of P percent, where the annual amount of the repayment is R dollars, paid at the end of each year. It stops after N years.

```
MORTGAG: PROCEDURE OPTIONS(MAIN);

    /*  PROGRAM TO COMPUTE REMAINING MORTGAGE              */
    /*   CURRENT MORTGAGE IS C, ANNUAL REPAYMENT IS R      */
    /*   PERCENTAGE IS       P, NUMBER OF YEARS IS  N      */
    /*   INPUT DATA CONSISTS OF INITIAL VALUES FOR         */
    /*   THESE VARIABLES IN THE ORDER SPECIFIED.           */

    DECLARE  (C, P, R) FLOAT DECIMAL,
             (N, I)   FIXED DECIMAL;
        GET LIST (C, R, P, N);
        I = 1;
        DO WHILE (I <= N);
            C = C*(1.0E0 + P*0.01E0) - R;
            PUT SKIP LIST ('AFTER YEAR',I,'LOAN BALANCE IS',C);
            I = I + 1;
            END;
    END MORTGAG;
```

Note that a new form of the PUT LIST statement has been used. The keyword SKIP has been added. This indicates that the information is to be printed starting on the next line. If SKIP is not present, PL/I prints the information on the end of the previous line, continuing in this way until a line is full. To see the difference, try running this program with and without the SKIP in the PUT LIST statement.

Another example is shown in Program P3.1, a PL/I version of the starship docking calculation from Chapter P3. This version prints the initial values and the result after each execution of the loop. Partial results of running this program with the input data

5.71, 2.0E6, 4.5, 500.0, 10.18, 205.0

are shown in Table P3.2.

Table 3.2 Sample run of Program P3.1

T	X	V
2.05000E+02	5.00000E+02	1.01799E+01
2.06000E+02	4.89819E+02	1.05011E+01
2.07000E+02	4.79318E+02	1.08100E+01
2.08000E+02	4.68508E+02	1.11061E+01
...	...	...
2.50000E+02	5.53487E+00	2.75149E+00
2.51000E+02	2.78338E+00	1.98345E+00
2.52000E+02	7.99930E-01	1.20453E+00
2.53000E+02	-4.04609E-01	4.17735E-01

Nested Loops

PL/I allows loops to be nested and labelled as in the text. Suppose, for example, that we want to print a table with ten rows of five columns. The first column should contain the numbers 1000, 2000, 3000, ..., 10000, while the Jth column should contain

Program P3.1 Starship Docking Calculation

```
STARDOK: PROCEDURE OPTIONS(MAIN);

    /*  PROGRAM TO COMPUTE DISTANCE FOR DOCKING.                 */
    /*  PROGRAM READS FOLLOWING REAL DATA VALUES:                */
    /*    G   GRAVITY FORCE OF BASE STATION                      */
    /*    C   COEFFICIENT OF REPULSIVE FORCE                     */
    /*    F   ENGINE THRUST                                      */
    /*    X   INITIAL DISTANCE FROM BASE STATION                 */
    /*    V   INITIAL VELOCITY OF STARSHIP                       */
    /*    T   INITIAL TIME                                       */

    DECLARE (G, C, F, X, V, T, NEXT_V ) FLOAT DECIMAL;
        GET LIST (G, C, F, X, V, T);
        PUT SKIP LIST ('T', 'X', 'V');
        PUT SKIP LIST (T, X, V);
        NEXT_V = V + G - F - C/(X + 1000.0)**2;
        DO WHILE (NEXT_V >= 0.0E0);
            /*      AT THIS POINT, NEXT_V CONTAINS THE           */
            /*      TIME  T + 1.0.                               */
            /*      THE LOOP ASSIGNS NEW VALUES TO T, V,         */
            /*      AND X.                                       */
            X = X - V;
            V = NEXT_V;
            T = T + 1.0;
            NEXT_V = V + G - F - C/(X + 1000.0)**2;
            PUT SKIP LIST (T, X, V);
            END;
    END STARDOK;
```

(10 + J*5) percent of the first column on the same row. The code below does this using two loops. The outer loop is labelled PRINT_ROW. The inner loop is not labelled in this example. Note that the expression used to compute VALUE has an additional 0.5E0 added to it. This causes the correct rounding when the value of the expression is converted to fixed point prior to assignment to VALUE.

```
TABLE: PROCEDURE OPTIONS(MAIN);
    DECLARE (I, J, VALUE) FIXED DECIMAL;
        I = 1000;
        PRINT_ROW: DO WHILE (I <= 10000);
            PUT SKIP LIST (I);
            J = 2;
            DO WHILE (J <= 5);
                VALUE = I * (10 + J*5) * 1E-2 + 0.5E0;
                PUT LIST (VALUE);
                J = J + 1;
                END;
            I = I + 1000;
            END PRINT_ROW;
    END TABLE;
```

Further Comments on Loops

PL/I has a form of DO statement that is used for counting loops; PL/I counting DO loops will be covered in detail in Section P8.1. However, txhe simple case of counting up through a number of values occurs so frequently, we will mention it here. The PL/I code

```
DO K = 1 TO N;
    PUT LIST (K);
    END;
```

prints the N integers 1, 2, ..., N. The PUT LIST statement in this example can be replaced with any sequence of statements. The sequence is then executed with K set to 1, 2, ..., up to N in order. For example, the code below prints a table of the squares and square roots of I for I = 1 to 20.

```
SQUARES: PROCEDURE OPTIONS(MAIN);
    DECLARE S FLOAT DECIMAL, (I, SQ) FIXED DECIMAL;
        PUT SKIP LIST ('I', 'SQUARE', 'SQUARE ROOT');
        DO I = 1 TO 20;
            SQ = I*I;
            S = SQRT(I);
            PUT SKIP LIST (I, SQ, S);
            END;
    END SQUARES;
```

Occasionally, we want to terminate a do-while loop on more than one condition. We have expressed this in the text by writing

do while condition-1 and condition-2

We write this in PL/I as

```
DO WHILE (condition-1 & condition-2)
```

The keyword and is simply replaced by the character "&" which means "and" in PL/I.

Loop Exits

In the text we introduced the concept of exitting from a loop when a condition occurred by writing

if condition then exit loop endif

In PL/I, this must be done using a combination of an IF statement and another statement called a GO TO statement. For example, the program structure

```
do forever
    first part of loop body
    if condition then exit loop endif
    rest of loop body
    enddo
```

can be coded in PL/I as

```
DO WHILE ('1'B);
    first part of loop body
    IF condition THEN GO TO label; ELSE;
    rest of loop body
    END;
label:
```

The first statement in this group means "do forever." ('1'B in PL/I is a condition that is always true. It is explained further in Chapter P9.) The GO TO keywords are followed by a "label" which is any valid name that must appear somewhere in front of a statement, and separated from that statement by a semi-colon. The effect of the GO TO is to cause the statement labelled with the same label to be executed next in sequence. Since the GO TO is executed only if the condition is true, the next statement executed is the labelled statement following the end of the loop if the condition is true, or the statement following the IF if the statement is false. Note that we have put the label immediately after the end of the loop. The reason for the "ELSE;" replacing the "endif" in our informal language will be explained in the next section.

If, for example, we want to read a sequence of values and print those values as long as they are positive, but stop the loop and print a termination message when the first negative value is read, we could write

```
DO WHILE ('1'B);
    GET LIST (V);
    IF V < 0 THEN GO TO READ_END; ELSE;
    PUT LIST (V);
    END;
READ_END:
PUT LIST ('END OF INPUT LIST REACHED');
```

The label used here is "READ_END"; it is a name similar to a variable name, but must not be identical to any variable name used in the program. Pxrogram P3.3 uses this construct in a square root calculation. This is a PL/I version of Program 3.3 in the text.

Program P3.3 Calculate Square Root

```
SQROOT: PROCEDURE OPTIONS(MAIN);
    /* PROGRAM TO READ A VALUE, X, AND COMPUTE ITS SQUARE ROOT */

    DECLARE (X, S_OLD, S) FLOAT DECIMAL;
        GET LIST(X);

        /*          COMPUTE FIRST APPROXIMATION  */
        S_OLD = (1.0E0 + X)*0.5E0;
        DO WHILE ('1'B);
            S = (S_OLD + X/S_OLD)*0.5E0;
            IF S > S_OLD THEN GO TO DONE; ELSE;
            S_OLD = S;
            END;
        DONE: PUT LIST ('SQUARE ROOT OF', X, 'IS', S);
    END SQROOT;
```

P3.2 If-then-else Statements

The PL/I if-then-else construct uses a form very similar to our informal language, but there are a number of differences that must be observed carefully. The basic PL/I construct is

```
IF condition
    THEN statement-1;
    ELSE statement-2;
```

If the condition is true, statement-1 is executed, otherwise statement-2 is executed. For example,

```
IF A > B
    THEN C = A;
    ELSE C = B;
```

sets C to be the larger of A or B. The _then_ and _else_ "clauses" are each one statement long in PL/I. There is no equivalent of the _endif_ of our informal language, but there is no need for it; the end of the _else_ clause is at the end of the first statement following the ELSE keyword. How, then, can we have more than one statement in a then or else clause, or no statements at all? It is easy to take care of no statements at all. For example, if we want to make A contain the larger of A and B we can write

```
IF A < B
   THEN A = B;
   ELSE;
```

The "null" else clause is indicated by a null statement, which in PL/I consists of nothing but the semi-colon ending the statement. It does nothing, as expected. (PL/I allows a null else statement to be omitted. However, it is not a good idea to omit it, as the presence of the ELSE keyword alerts us to the end of the IF.)

Compound Statements

If we want to include more than one statement in a then or else clause in a PL/I program, we must use a _compound statement_. A compound statement is a sequence of statements between the pair of keywords DO and END. Thus

```
DO;
   statement-a;
   statement-b;
   statement-c
   END;
```

is a group of three statements that make one compound statement. The DO statement without any additional qualifiers does not cause repeated execution of the block of statements between it and its matching END statement, rather it creates a single group that is executed once. For example, if we want to switch the values of A and B if A is smaller than B we can write

```
IF A < B
   THEN DO; T = A; A = B; B = T; END;
   ELSE;
```

The correct way to view the DO group in PL/I is as a compound statement that is executed under the control of the DO. If the keyword DO is not qualified, the compound statement is executed just once; otherwise it is executed as many times as specified.

An IF statement, with its _then_ and _else_ clauses, is also a compound statement, so it can appear as the statement in a then or else clause of a larger IF statement. For example, if we want to increment N1, N2, or N3 by 1, depending whether the value of A is negative, zero, or positive, we can write

```
IF A < 0
    THEN N1 = N1 + 1;
    ELSE IF A = 0
            THEN N2 = N2 + 1;
            ELSE N3 = N3 + 1;
```

P3.2 If-then-else Statements

Program P3.5 is a PL/I version of Program 3.5. It initially sets the variable L to zero, for a non-leap year. L is set to one if the year is determined to be a leap year.

Program P3.5 Leap Year Calculation

```
LEAP_YR: PROCEDURE OPTIONS(MAIN);
    /*  AN INTEGER YEAR NUMBER IS READ.  THE PROGRAM  */
    /*  DETERMINES IF THE YEAR IS A LEAP YEAR.        */

    DECLARE (L, Y) FIXED DECIMAL;
        L = 0;
        GET LIST (Y);
        IF TRUNC(Y/4.0E0)*4 = Y
            THEN IF TRUNC(Y/100.0E0)*100 = Y
                    THEN IF TRUNC(Y/400.0E0)*400 = Y
                            THEN L = 1;
                            ELSE L = 0;
                    ELSE L = 1;
            ELSE L = 0;
        IF L = 0
            THEN PUT LIST ('YEAR', Y, 'IS NOT A LEAP YEAR');
            ELSE PUT LIST ('YEAR', Y, 'IS A LEAP YEAR');
    END LEAP_YR;
```

PL/I Precedence Rules for Relational Operators.

The relational operators given in Table P3.1 follow the precedence rules given in Chapter P3, namely, they have lower precedence than the arithmetic operators. For example, we can write "A+B > C", which is true if A+B is greater than C. Similarly, "A + B > 0.0" is the same as "A > -B", "-A < B", or "0.0 > -A -B".

Problems

1. The program to compute remaining mortgage balance earlier in this chapter computes the quantity (1.0E0 + P*0.01E0) every time that the loop is executed. This is inefficient. Reprogram it so the the calculation is done only once.

2. Write a program to find both roots of a quadratic equation. If the discriminant B**2 - 4.0E0*A*C is negative, print the a line containing

   REAL PART IS x IMAGINARY PART IS y

   where x and y are the values of -B/(2.0E0*A) and SQRT(-B**2 + 4.0E0*A*C)/(2.0E0*A) respectively; otherwise, print the two real roots given by

   (-B + SQRT(B**2 - 4.0E0*A*C))/(2.0E0*A)
   and (-B - SQRT(B**2 - 4.0E0*A*C))/(2.0E0*A)

Program in text to convert to PL/I: P3.2

Problem in text to do in PL/I: 5.

P4 ARRAYS

An array is declared in PL/I following the general principle used in the pseudolanguage: the dimensions are given following the declaration of the name. For example,

```
DECLARE  (SCORE(20), W(8), GRADE(150)) FLOAT DECIMAL;
```

declares the three names SCORE, W, and GRADE to be the names of arrays of 20, 8, and 150 elements respectively. As in the text, they can be referenced by writing, for example, SCORE(15) to refer to the fifteenth element of SCORE.

Example

The sum GRADE(1) + GRADE(2) + ... + GRADE(150) can be formed by executing

```
SUM = 0;
DO I = 1 TO 150;
    SUM = SUM + GRADE(I);
    END;
```

(Of course, it could be formed by writing an expression using each of the 150 elements of GRADE and 149 addition signs, but that is hardly an elegant or concise form!)

The index used to reference an array can be an arbitrary expression. The expression is evaluated and converted to an integers to determine the actual reference. For example, a reference to SCORE(3.25*3) is the same as a reference to SCORE(9).

Example

The following section of code switches the order of the elements B(1) to B(N) in the array B. B is assumed to be dimensioned earlier in the program.

```
DO I = 1 TO N/2;
    TEMP = B(N+1-I);
    B(N+1-I) = B(I);
    B(I) = TEMP;
    END;
```

The dimension of an array can also be an expression. Obviously it must have a value which can be calculated. The integer part of this value is taken as the dimension. Thus

```
DECLARE TEMPERATURE(2*2*3.7) FLOAT DECIMAL;
```

is the same as

```
DECLARE TEMPERATURE(14) FLOAT DECIMAL;
```

At this stage, the dimension of an array will always be a constant, but in Chapters P7 and P10 we will see applications in which the dimensions can be expressions involving variables computed during a previous part of the calculation. The important point to note now is that at the point the declaration is made, the value of the expression is computed, and space is allocated for all of the array elements.

In the text, our array subscripts are limited to values between 1 and the upper limit of the particular dimension. PL/I relaxes this restriction, and allows a lower limit to be specified also. For example,

```
DECLARE (TEMP(-2:2), SCORE(0:100), X(3:5))FLOAT DECIMAL;
```

declares three arrays. The first, TEMP, has 5 elements, TEMP(-2), TEMP(-1), TEMP(0), TEMP(1), and TEMP(2); the second, SCORE, has 101 elements; the third, X, has 3 elements, X(3) though X(5). The lower and upper bounds can both be expressions. Their values, after conversion to integers, must be such that the lower bound does not exceed the upper bound. For example, a declaration of B(5:4) is invalid.

P4.1 Higher Dimensional Arrays

PL/I allows many dimensions to be used, but the user should be aware that it is possible to use large amounts of memory if very many dimensions are used. For example, the declaration

```
DECLARE TEMP(100,100,100) FLOAT DECIMAL;
```

uses one million words of memory, an amount not available on many computer systems.

Arrays in PL/I are stored by row, so that if an array B is declared by B(n1,n2,n3) where n1, n2 and n3 are integers, the address of B(I,J,K) is
B + I-1 + n1*(J-1 + n2*(K-1)), where B is the address of B(1,1,1). The last index in a PL/I multi-dimensional array varies most rapidly as consecutive cells in memory are addressed.

Program P4.2 is a PL/I version of Program P4.2. The programmer should be aware that computer time is consumed in indexing when the index is other than a constant. The statement SUM(I) = SUM(I) + SCORE(I,J)*W(J) is executed N*M times, once for each pass through the inner loop. However, I does not change in the inner loop, so that the variable SUM(I) refers to a single cell in memory for M consecutive executions of the inner loop. For this reason, it is better to replace the body of the outer loop with the section of code in program P4.2a. The additional variable S, which should be declared as a real, is used to form the weighted sum of scores, and finally its value is assigned to SUM(I).

Program P4.2 Use of One- and Two-dimensional Arrays

```
WT_SCOR: PROCEDURE OPTIONS(MAIN);

    /*  COMPUTE WEIGHTED SUM OF SCORES                        */
    /*  SCORE, W, N, AND M MUST BE SET BY ADDITIONAL CODE     */

    DECLARE (I, J, N, M)             FIXED DECIMAL,
        (SCORE(150,8), W(8), SUM(150))  FLOAT DECIMAL;

        OUTER: DO I = 1 TO N;
            SUM(I) = 0.0;
            INNER: DO J = 1 TO M;
                SUM(I) = SUM(I) + SCORE(I,J)*W(J);
                END INNER;
            END OUTER;
    END WT_SCOR;
```

Program P4.2a Change to Program P4.2a for Efficiency

```
S = 0.0;
INNER: DO J = 1 TO M;
    S = S + SCORE(I,J)*W(J);
    END INNER:
SUM(I) = S;
```

Program P4.2 labels the two loops with the names OUTER and INNER. These labels may then appear in the END statements matching the DO statements with the same labels. These have no effect on the program, but they do make it easier to read.

Any of the dimension specifications of a multi-dimensional array may be specified as a lower:upper bound pair. For example,

```
DECLARE (BB(0:100,-5:5), DD(10,-4:5)) FLOAT DECIMAL;
```

declares BB to be an array of 1111 (= 101 * 11) elements, and DD to be an array of 100 elements.

Problems

1. How many elements are there in the array Z if the declaration is

   a. Z(5,10)
   b. Z(-9:15)
   c. Z(-10:0,0:100)
   d. Z(4:5,5,6)

2. If B(1,1) is in memory location 1936, in which location is B(17,13) if B is declared as

   a. B(50,20)
   b. B(17,18)
   c. B(20,13)
   d. B(-10:10,5)
   e. B(-2:17,0:20)

   Assume that each element of B occupies one word in memory.

3. Write a PL/I program to transpose a two-dimensional square array B. A two-dimensional square array is one in which the first and second dimensions have the same size. Suppose they are both 1:N. A transpose of B is an array C such that C(J,I) = B(I,J).

4. Write a PL/I program that will transpose B (as in problem 2) *in situ*, that is, change the elements of B so that the new value of B is the transpose of the old value.

5. A matrix is a two-dimensional array. The product of a pair of matrices A and B is defined to be a matrix C such that

   ```
   C(I,K) = A(I,1)*B(1,K) + A(I,2)*B(2,K) + ... + A(I,N)*B(N,K)
   ```

   for all I and K. Assuming that A is M by N (that is, that the first dimension of A is 1:M and the second 1:N), and that B is N by L, write a section of PL/I code to compute the M by L matrix C which is the matrix product of A and B.

Programs in text to convert to PL/I: P4.1, P4.3.

Problems in text to do in PL/I: 5, 6, 7, and 8.

P5 DEBUGGING PL/I AND PL/C PROGRAMS

Debugging a program in a particular language is part art and part science. The algorithm and the program structure should be designed carefully so that it is possible to check that the algorithm works for the problem. Before the algorithm can be checked completely on the computer, however, it is necessary to check that the coded form implements the intended algorithm. This can be the most difficult step.

Debugging techniques are very dependent on the compiler and system used. Some systems provide a lot of diagnostic facilities; others do little more than announce that there has been an execution-time error. Fortunately, the PL/I language was designed with the problem of debugging in mind, so it has a number of features that make error detection and isolation easy for some types of errors. These features have been enhanced in PL/C. We will describe some general techniques that can be used in PL/I and some of the special techniques available in PL/C.

Syntax Errors

The first step is to remove the syntax errors. This is not too difficult because they are detected by the compiler and usually isolated down to particular statements. Most compilers number the lines or statements in the program and indicate the offending lines by number. (See, for example, Figure G1.1.) Some errors will cause an error indication in later lines that are not in error. For example, failure to dimension a variable will cause the compiler to think that a reference to a variable such as B(I) is a use of a function B(I) -- similar to SQRT(A) or other functions, and an error will be detected when an assignment such as "B(I) = 1;" is compiled. A little experience with any particular compiler will usually make the programmer aware of the causes of common error messages of this type. Mistyped statements can cause apparently ridiculous error messages, but if the offending statement is isolated, the programmer can simply check the syntax of the statement carefully against the rules. For example, a statement such as

```
DOI = 1 TO N;
```

might produce an error message indicating that there is a semicolon missing. This would happen if the compiler first recognizes the three characters DOI as an identifier (a space must appear around keywords in PL/I) and then assumes that it is reading an assignment statement. When it reaches the keyword TO, it thinks that there should have been a semicolon after the number 1 to complete the assignment statement.

The most common cause of difficult-to-understand syntax errors in PL/C is the use of a reserved word as an identifier. If you cannot understand an error message, check the list of reserved words (under keywords in Chapter C1). Another common error in PL/I or PL/C is use of the wrong card columns. Normally, information in column 1 and columns 73 to 80 is ignored. If, for example, the character or characters terminating a statement appear beyond column 72, the statement will be thought to continue to the next line by the compiler. This can cause strange error messages. Check the statement numbers that appear on the left-hand side of the page carefully to see if the compiler has grouped several statements together.

Semantic errors (errors in the meaning rather than the structure) are not usually detected by the compiler, although some compilers such as PL/C do a better job than others.

Mispunching is a cause of many errors. If these cause syntactic errors, they are detected, but frequently a variable name is misspelled. This type of error can be detected in languages which require all variables to be declared, unless the misspelling changes the name to the name of another variable that is also used. For this reason, it is wise to avoid using similar names, such as SUM and SVM. It is particularly important to avoid variables that differ only in the use of zero and the letter O, or one and the letter I, because it is very easy to mistake AO for A0 or ZI for Z1. Unfortunately, PL/I does not require all variables to be declared, so misspelling a variable name may result in the default declaration of another variable. Some compilers print a list of all variables used. If one is available, it is worthwhile looking through the list to see if there are any names present that were not intended to be used. Most PL/I compilers indicate where the variable was declared, and you can use this to detect the fact that it was not declared. In PL/C, you should specify the ATR option on the $PLC card to get a listing of all variables used. (See Chapter C4.)

Run-time Errors

Detection of run-time errors is partly a function of the compiler and partly a function of the operating system (see Section C5.2). Almost all systems detect major errors such as overflow, attempts to use non-existent memory and invalid machine instructions. Some compilers generate internal forms of the program that detect language independent errors. Examples of these errors include

Out-of-range index in dimensioned variable
Use of the value of a variable before a value has been assigned

If these are not detected, an error will appear later in the program. The sooner in the execution of a program an error can be detected, the easier it is to isolate that error. If several errors are detected, start looking for the one that apparently occurred first.

The first step in looking for the error is to read the section of code carefully. If the behavior of the program cannot be understood, the next step is to run the program to get additional output. The data-directed output statement PUT DATA(...); is very useful for this purpose. For example, PUT DATA(A,I,K,X); prints the values of A, I, K and X together with their names, so that the programmer does not have to output additional identification. This statement is described in Chapter P6. In addition, PL/C provides special versions of the PUT statement for diagnostic "dumping" of the values of variables. They are "PUT ALL" which prints the values of every simple variable currently defined. It is equivalent to a PUT DATA (...) listing every simple variable. PUT ARRAY is similar, but it also outputs the values of all arrays currently in use.

The CHECK Prefix

PL/I provides additional powerful facilities for examining the values of variables during the execution of the program. The CHECK prefix allows variables to be "flagged" so that each time their value is changed, they are printed. The CHECK prefix appears before the definition of a procedure, and is written "(CHECK(variable list)):" For example, when the program

```
(CHECK(A, I, SUM)):
MAIN: PROCEDURE OPTIONS (MAIN);
    DECLARE (A, SUM, Z) FLOAT DECIMAL, I FIXED DECIMAL;
    SUM = 0.0E0; Z = 0.0E0;
    SUM_LOOP: DO I = 1 TO 5;
        GET LIST (A);
        SUM = SUM + A;
        Z = Z + SUM;
        END SUM_LOOP;
    END MAIN;
```

is executed, the values of A, I and SUM are printed each time they are changed, that is every time a value is read into A, every time I is changed in the loop, and every time SUM is assigned a value. It is as if a PUT DATA(variable name) has been placed immediately after each statement that changes one of the variables named. This can generate a lot of output, so you should not CHECK variables of little interest.

The CHECK prefix can also be used to monitor the execution of sections of code. This is done by including the label of a statement in the prefix list. Thus, if the identifier SUM_LOOP is added to the list in the example above, the name SUM_LOOP is printed each time the DO statement is executed. PL/I allows labels to be prefixed to any executable statement (a label is an identifier followed by a colon appearing in front of a statement) so that the sections of code being executed can be identified easily. (In PL/C, but not PL/I, there are special statements CHECK and NOCHECK that turn the checking on and off. Executing the statement NOCHECK disables the checking indicated for the procedure until the statement CHECK is executed. The CHECK statement may also include a parameter indicating the number of times that the value of the variable is to be printed. Thus, the statement CHECK(5); indicates that the variables indicated in the CHECK prefix are to be printed five times maximum until another CHECK statement is executed. A limiting of the effect of the CHECK prefix can be obtained in PL/I by use of the BEGIN block discussed in Chapter P10. A CHECK prefix can be applied to a BEGIN block, in which case it does not apply to code external to that block.)

Flow Tracing

As long as the program follows a known path, it can be checked step by step by using intermediate output statements. The intermediate values of variables should be checked to see if they satisfy the assertions that are supposed to be true. If a program gets "stuck" in a loop, it may be necessary to output intermediate data values for every pass through the loop to determine why the termination condition is not being met. These methods will eventually enable the programmer to find the errors.

Unfortunately, occasionally a program will behave in a way that seems to defy explanation. It will not follow the expected path and will stop for some unexplained condition. The first step should be to determine the path of the program. The CHECK prefix described above can be used for this purpose by attaching labels to various section of code. For example, if you want to find out whether a then or else clause is executed for a particular statement, you can add labels to them in the form

```
IF condition
   THEN LABEL1: DO;
      then clause
        END;
    ELSE LABEL2: DO;
        else clause
        END;
```

If the labels LABEL1 and LABEL2 are included in the CHECK prefix list, the output will tell you which clause is executed each time the IF is executed.

PL/C provides a special FLOW feature that allows the programmer to request information about the flow of the program during execution. The keyword FLOW is both a prefix and a statement. If a procedure is to be monitored for program flow, the characters (FLOW): must appear before the procedure statement. In addition, the statement FLOW must be executed inside the procedure. The statement FLOW turns on the output of the flow trace. If it is not executed, the output remains off. It can be turned back off with the NOFLOW statement. When the FLOW prefix has been specified and the output has been turned on by the FLOW statement, PL/C prints a terse indication of the flow of control every time that a statement which can change control flow is executed. These include IF statements, and the ends of DO loops. For example, if flow printing is on, and the statement

```
23      IF A > B
24          THEN C = D;
25          ELSE E = F;
```

is executed, where the numbers 23 to 25 are the statements numbers assigned by PL/C in the program listing, PL/C will print either "23->24" or "23->25", meaning that either the execution of statement 23 lead to the execution of statement 24, or that the execution of statement 23 lead to the execution of statement 25.

A DO loop causes flow trace printing to occur each time the loop is repeated and when it is terminated. For example,

```
36      I = N;
37      DO WHILE (I > 0);
...         body of loop
51          I = I + 1;
52          END;
53      ...
```

will generate the output 52->37 N times, once for each completion of the loop. (If the statements in the body of the loop generate no output, this will be printed as N*(52->37), where N is replaced by its integer value.) Finally, the output 37->53 will be generated.

<u>Termination</u>

If the program stops abruptly for a reason that is hard to understand, it is important to try and find the real reason for the termination. Usually the system prints the reason for the termination of the job, and this may provide an important clue to the error. If, for example, it is due to an attempt to take the square root of a negative number, the system will indicate where the problem occurred in the program. The programmer can check back from that point, examining the values of various data values. Other reasons for termination do not provide much information about the error. An attempt to use memory not allocated to the program, for example, can be caused by an out-of-range index, in which case isolation may be easy, but it can be caused by an earlier out-of-range index which overwrote a part of the program.

Fortunately, PL/I makes it possible to determine when an out-of-range subscript is used. The condition SUBSCRIPTRANGE can be used as a prefix to a statement or a procedure. If, for example, we write (SUBSCRIPTRANGE): in front of the main procedure definition, the compiled program will print an error message if any subscript is out of range. This is a powerful diagnostic facility, and should always be used during program debugging unless there are very strong reasons for not using it. It can be disabled for a single statement or procedure by prefixing the statement or procedure with the condition NOSUBSCRIPTRANGE. (Fortunately, PL/C has this condition normally enabled.)

PL/I has many other conditions which can optionally cause error printing and/or termination of execution. Some of these are OVERFLOW, FIXEDOVERFLOW, UNDERFLOW, and ZERODIVIDE, which detect floating-point overflow, fixed-point overflow, floating-point underflow, and an attempted division by zero respectively. All of these conditions are normally enabled. That is, if the situation arises, a error print occurs and execution may terminate. (PL/C attempts to continue execution with some sort of fix-up of the error, while PL/I usually terminates execution.) These conditions can be disabled by using a prefix consisting of the word preceded by NO. For example,

```
(SUBSCRIPTRANGE, NOUNDERFLOW):
MM: PROCEDURE OPTIONS(MAIN);
```

will allow the procedure to continue if an underflow occurs, but it will be terminated if a subscript is out of range.

P6 INPUT/OUTPUT IN PL/I

Until now, we have been using simple list-directed input/output. PL/I provides the two additional forms of input/output called _edit-directed_ and _data-directed_. The principles of these forms are discussed in the text. In this chapter we will give additional facts about PL/I list directed I/O, and then cover edit- and data-directed I/O. Finally, we will mention some additional features available in PL/I input/output.

PL/I list-directed input/output is similar to that used in the text. It is written in the form

```
        GET LIST (list);
and     PUT LIST (list);
```

where _list_, called the I/O list, is a list of variable names or array elements whose values are to be input or output. If the option SKIP is used by writing, for example,

```
PUT SKIP LIST (A, B);
```

a new line is started and the values of A and B are printed. This is similar to the I/O described in the text. However, if SKIP is not specified, the values to be output are placed on the end of the previous line, as long as there is space. For example,

```
PUT SKIP LIST(A, B, C, D);
PUT LIST (E, F, G);
```

will start a new line of output, and then print the values of A, B, C, and D on that line. The second statement will continue on the same line, printing the value of E. However, on most systems, space is allocated for five fields on a single line, and each field can contain no more than one value. (In PL/C the fields are 24 character spaces long.) Consequently, the second statement will continue to the next line, and put the values of F and G in the first two fields on that line.

Vertical page control is obtained by using the options SKIP, PAGE, and LINE. We have just seen that SKIP skips to the beginning of the next line. This is the same as specifying SKIP(1). If we specify SKIP(e), where e is any expression (including a constant such as 3, the expression is evaluated, converted to an integer, and that many lines are skipped. Thus, SKIP(4.6), which is the sams as SKIP(4), generates three blank lines and starts printing on the fourth. The option PAGE cause the next line to be started on the first line at the top of the next page, while LINE(e) causes the next line to be started at the e-th line of the page -- e is evaluated, converted to an integer, and used to control the output of blank lines. For example, suppose that the current line is being printed on the 17th line of the page. PUT LINE(33) LIST (X); will print the value of X on the 33rd line by outputting 15 blank lines and then outputting X. On the other hand, PUT LINE(5) LIST (X); will eject the paper to the top the the next page, then output 4 blank lines so that X is printed on the 5-th line of the new page -- it does not back up the paper to an earlier line!

The I/O list in the PUT statement consists of a number of items separated from each other with commas. These items can be constants, variables, array elements, expressions, or compound data items such as array names. The value, or values, of each item are printed in successive fields, five to a line. If an array name appears, each element in the array is output in row order. Thus, if the declaration of Z's dimensions is Z(-1:1,0:1), the elements Z(-1,0), Z(-1,1), Z(0,0), and Z(0,1) are output. An item can consist of a character string such as 'OUTPUT THIS'. The characters in the string are output without the surrounding quotes. If a quote is needed, two adjacent quotes must be used in the string.

An implicit DO loop can be specified in an I/O list. For example,

```
PUT LIST (X, (W(I) DO I = 3 TO 10));
```

outputs 9 values, X, and W(3) to W(10). These implicit loops can be nested. For example, to output the elements of Z(-1:0,0:1) in column order we can write

```
PUT LIST ( ((Z(I,J) DO I = -1 TO 0) DO J = 0 TO 1));
```

List-directed input is very similar to list-directed output except that the I/O list may not contain expressions or constants. Successive values are read from the input. Each value must be separated from the previous one by a comma and/or one or more blanks. If there are insufficient values on the current input line to provide values for all of the items in the input list, a new line is started. If there are too many values on the line, the unused ones are not read; they are left for the next input. However, by specifying SKIP in the GET statement, the input automatically begins at the start of the next line. For example

```
GET SKIP LIST (A, B, C);
GET LIST (D, E, F);
GET SKIP LIST (X);
```

reads seven values. Suppose that these are the first GET statements to be used to read from the input. The first two statements are identical to the single statement

```
GET SKIP LIST (A, B, C, D, E, F);
```

They read six values from as many lines as necessary to obtain six values. If, for example, the first line contains four values and the second three, A through D are assigned values from the first line, while E and F are assigned the first two values from the second line. The third GET statement begins reading the third line. If the second line had only contained two values, the third GET statement would still read from the third line as the SKIP only causes data to be skipped if a line has not been completely read.

The data to be read by a GET LIST statement can appear in any reasonable way, with or without exponents, with or without a decimal point, and with or without a sign. On input, the values are converted to the appropriate representation, as determined by the type of the data in the input list. For example, if a line contains

```
23.4E3, -45, 123.456   543  6E-1
```

the statement

```
GET LIST (A, I, J, B, Z);
```

will perform the equivalent of the five assignments

```
A = 23.4E3; I = -45; J = 123.456; B = 543; Z = 6E-1;
```

with whatever conversion they imply.

P6 INPUT/OUTPUT IN PL/I

P6.1 Edit-Directed I/O

This type of input/output allows the format of the external data to be specified. For example, we might want to state that three single digit integers are to be read from columns one through three of the next line. This can be done by executing

```
GET SKIP EDIT (I, J, K) (F(1), F(1), F(1));
```

The format appears inside parentheses following the I/O list. In this case, the format descriptor is F, standing for Fixed point. F(1) means a fixed point number with one character. Each of the three entries in the format specification describes a one character fixed point number. The first descriptor is used to describe the first entry in the I/O list, the second descriptor the second entry, and so on. If, for example, we had wished to read J from a two-column field, but I and K from one-columns fields, we should have executed

```
GET SKIP EDIT (I, J, K) (F(1), F(2), F(1));
```

The value read under control of the F format descriptor must be a fixed point number, that is, it may contain a decimal point and an initial sign, but it must not contain any embedded blanks or an exponent. If the data type of the item in the I/O list is not fixed point, the value will be converted. Thus

```
GET SKIP EDIT (A) (F(10));
```

will read the first ten columns of the next line. If they contain bbb-67.34b, where b is a blank character, and if A is a floating point variable, A is assigned the value -0.6734E+2. On the other hand, if A is a fixed-point variable declared by FIXED DECIMAL, it is assigned the value -67.

On output, the F descriptor causes a fixed point number to be printed, regardless of the type of data in the I/O list. The data is first converted to fixed point (rounded if necessary), and then printed in the number of columns indicated. For example, F(9) prints an integer in nine columns. The number is right justified in the field, and preceded by a minus sign if negative. Thus,

```
PUT SKIP EDIT (45.6, -374 ) (F(3), F(6));
```

will print b46bb-374 in the first nine columns of the next line.

The F format descriptor can also specify the position of a decimal point in the input or output. The descriptor F(7,3) specifies that three decimal digits should appear after the decimal point. Thus

```
PUT EDIT (45678E-4, -123) (F(10,3), F(6,1));
```

prints the characters bbbbb4.568b-123.0 on the end of the current line. (Note that if SKIP is not specified, each PUT adds characters to the current line.) On input, the format descriptor F(10.3) indicates that the point should be to the left of the last three digits. If the input value includes a decimal point, this is ignored. Otherwise the point is assumed to be there. For example, if A is floating point, and the next 10 input characters are bbbb+45678, the statement

```
GET EDIT (A) (F(10,3));
```

will assign .45678E2 to A.

Three other format descriptors for data are important to us right now, the E-field, the X-field, and the A-field descriptors. E specified a floating-point format. E(w,d) specifies that a number to be printed should have d digits after the decimal point, occupy w columns, and include an exponent. For example, E(12,4) causes the the number -0.00453826 to be printed as ƀ-4.5383E-03. Since one column may be used for the sign (it is not printed if the number is positive), one is used for a digit in front of the decimal point, one is used for the decimal point, d are used for the digits after the point, and four are used for the exponent, w should be at least d+7. Sufficient blanks are added to the left to fill up the field. The E format also allows the number of digits in front of the point to be specified. This is done with a third entry in the parentheses. E(w,d,s) causes a number to be printed in a w-column field with s-d digits in front of the decimal point, d digits after, a sign if negative, and an exponent. Thus, s is the total number of significant digits printed. For example, E(15,3,5) will cause the number .234567E-2 to be printed as ƀƀƀƀ23.457E-04. If this option is used, w must be at least s+6. Note that E(w,d) is the same as E(w,d,d+1). On input, a value is read from a w-column field. The value read may have a sign and/or an exponent, although neither is necessary. If it has a decimal point, both d and s in the E(w,d,s) format are ignored, otherwise the point is assumed to be to the left of the rightmost d digits of the mantissa and s is ignored.

The X field descriptor describes a field that is ignored on input and filled with blanks on output. X(5) specifies five blank columns. For example,

```
PUT SKIP EDIT (M,N) (F(5),X(15),F(7));
```

prints the values of M and N in columns 1 through 5 and 21 through 27 respectively. On input, X(w) causes the next w columns to be ignored.

The A-field descriptor specifies an alphanumeric field, that is, one containing characters. We saw that we can output a string of characters by enclosing them in quotes and placing them in the I/O list. If the EDIT option is used we must indicate how many columns are to be used for the characters. A(w) specifies a w-character field. The statement

```
PUT SKIP EDIT ('VALUE OF N IS ', N) (A(20),F(5));
```

will print the line

```
VALUE OF N IS       -1234
```

if N has the value indicated. The string 'VALUE OF N IS ' has been placed in the left hand side of a 20-column field. The 5-column field containing N starts in column 21. If the field for the string had been too short, the string would have been truncated. If, for example, the descriptor had been A(7),F(5), the output would have been "VALUE 0-1234". The field length can been omitted from an A-field descriptor, in which case the length of the string provided is used. For example, if we used the descriptor A,F(5) in the PUT statement above, the output would be "VALUE OF N IS -2345". Use of the A descriptor for input will be covered in Chapter P9 when we discuss character strings.

The keywords PAGE, SKIP, and LINE can be used as part of format descriptors. They cause their usual action at the time they are processed, rather than at the start of the PUT or GET statement. For example,

```
PUT EDIT (A, B, C) (E(12,3),PAGE,LINE(5),F(10,2),SKIP(2),E12,5);
```

causes A to be printed on the current line, B to be printed on the beginning of the 5th line of the next page, and C to be printed on the start of the 7th line of that page.

One additional keyword that is very useful for printing is COLUMN. COLUMN(16) indicates that the next descriptor is to start in column 16. If column 16 of the current line has already been passed, then processing of the next line is begun. For example,

```
PUT SKIP EDIT ('STUDENT', GRADE-POINT', 'NAME', 'AVERAGE')
              (COLUMN(5),A,COLUMN(30),A,COLUMN(5),A,COLUMN(30),A);
```

causes the two lines

```
STUDENT                  GRADE-POINT
NAME                     AVERAGE
```

to be printed.

Frequently we wish to repeat a single format descriptor or a group of descriptors. If, for example, we wished to specify five 7-character fixed point fields, we can write 5F(7). If we wished to specify a sequence of six lines, each containing a fixed-point and a floating point number, we can write 6(F(5),E(12,5)). Note that the group is enclosed in parentheses, and the repetition count precedes the group. A group of specifications enclosed in parentheses can appear in place of a single specification statement, so that we can write compound specifications such as 3(F(4),2(A(2)),E(10,3), which is the same as F(4),A(2),A(2),F(4),A(2),...,A(2),E(10,3).

Any of the integer constants appearing in format specifiers can be expressions. These are evaluated each time the specifier is needed. For example,

```
PUT EDIT (I DO I = 1 TO 6) (6(SKIP, F(I));
```

causes the output

```
1
 2
  3
   4
    5
     6
```

(Note that numerical output is right-justified in the print field, whereas character output is left-justified.)

P6.2 Data-Directed Output

Data-directed I/O is much as described in the text. Use of data-directed input is not recommended, so we will discuss only the output form here.

```
PUT DATA (list)
```

outputs the values of the variables given in the list together with the names of the variables. Thus

```
PUT SKIP DATA (A, B)
```

will output

```
A = 3.45678E-03      B =       -1234
```

if A is FLOAT and B is FIXED. Note that the elements of the list <u>must</u> be variable names:

expressions are not allowed in data-directed output. The SKIP option can be omitted with the usual result--printing continues on the end of the previous line.

6.3 Other I/O Considerations

PL/I allows the file for input and output to be specified in the GET and PUT statements. For example,

```
GET FILE (SYSIN) LIST (A, B, C);
```

specifies that values of the variables A, B, and C are to be read from the file named SYSIN. SYSIN is the _default_ file for a GET statement, just as SYSOUT is the default file for a PUT statement, so it is not necessary to specify it. However, if data were stored on another file, say SOURCE, the file specification FILE(SOURCE) should be included with the GET statement. It is also necessary to _open_ the file before it is used with the OPEN statement. For example,

```
OPEN FILE (SOURCE) INPUT;
```

specifies that the file named SOURCE is to be made available as an INPUT file so that it can be referenced in a later GET statement. The location of the file of data in the system must also be specified; unfortunately, this is a system dependent matter, and is beyond the scope of an introductory treatment. We will restrict ourselves to use of SYSIN and SYSOUT, which are automatically allocated space and opened for us.

Detecting End-of-File

In earlier examples, we have used a particular data value to indicate the end of a set of input data. If a program attempts to read beyond the end of the input data, a condition called _end-of-file_ occurs. If no action is taken by the programmer to handle the condition, the program is aborted. PL/I allows the programmer to specify what is to happen when an end-of-file occurs on a particular unit in an ON statement. The form of this is

```
ON ENDFILE (SYSIN) <ON-unit>;
```

where <ON-unit> is the action to be taken if an end-of-file occurs on the indicated unit (SYSIN in this example). We will use a GO TO statement as the ON-unit in our examples as shown in the code below, which reads up to 100 values into the array X, exitting the loop if an end-of-file is detected before 100 elements have been read.

```
ON ENDFILE (SYSIN) GO TO L1_END;
DO I = 1 TO 100;
    GET LIST (A(I)); /* IF END-OF-FILE THEN EXIT LOOP */
    END;
L1_END:
```

P6 INPUT/OUTPUT IN PL/I

Problems

1. Write edit-directed I/O statements to do each of the following. Allow for 5 digits after the point in reals.

   a. Input an integer from columns 1 to 5, a real from columns 11 to 20, and an integer from columns 25 to 30.
   b. Output an integer in columns 2 to 4, followed by 5 reals, each occupying 15 columns, starting in column 10.
   c. Output 50 integers, printed 10 per line, 5 columns each.
   d. Output 20 pairs of numbers, each pair consisting of a 5 column integer and a 15 column real, with 5 pairs per line.

2. Write a formatted output statement to print the Ith row of an N by M array of integers, assuming that 10 columns can be used for each entry and that there are 100 columns on the printer.

3. What is printed if the statement

```
PUT EDIT (('TABLE',I,(J DO J = 1 TO 5) DO I = 1 TO 5)) (<format>);
```

   is executed, where <format> is the string

```
(a)  PAGE,A,5(SKIP, F(5),5F(3))
(b)  PAGE, LINE(2), A(10), 5(SKIP,F(3),COLUMN(9),5F(3))
(c)  A(0), 6(SKIP,6F(3))
(d)  PAGE, LINE(2), A(10), 5(SKIP,F(3),X(10),COLUMN(9),5F(3))
```

4. What does the statement below output?

```
PUT LIST ('X','X','X','X','X','X','X','X','X','X')
        (SKIP,2(X(3),2A(2),X(1),A,X(1),2A(3)));
```

P7 PROCEDURES

PL/I uses the name PROCEDURE to refer to a main program or subprogram. We have already seen that the main program is preceded by the keywords PROCEDURE OPTIONS(MAIN) and followed by the keyword END. Subprograms are similarly bracketted with the keywords PROCEDURE and END.

PL/I has many built-in function procedures such as MAX and SQRT. A number of these are listed in Chapter C3. They fall into four main classes:

arithmetic
mathematical
array
string

The built-in arithmetic functions operate on an argument of any arithmetic type, and, in almost all cases, return a result of the same type. Thus, ABS(X) is the absolute value of X. If X is FLOAT DECIMAL, then X is also FLOAT DECIMAL, so that ABS(-34E5) is 34E5. If X is FIXED DECIMAL, then ABS(X) is also FIXED DECIMAL. Thus ABS(-654) is 654. The arithmetic functions MIN and MAX return a result which is the "highest" type of all arguments--that is, if any argument is FLOAT, the result is FLOAT.

The built-in mathematical functions such as SQRT expect a FLOAT argument. If the argument is not a floating-point value, it is converted to one. Thus, SQRT(45) is the same as SQRT(45E0). The result has the same type as the argument after conversion, that is, FLOAT.

Arithmetic and mathematical built-in functions can be used on array arguments, in which case the operation is performed on every element of the array. For example,

```
DECLARE (Y(10,5), Z(10,5)) FLOAT DECIMAL;
    ... set values in array Z
    Y = SQRT(Z);
```

sets all 50 elements of Y to the square roots of the corresponding elements of Z. That is, it is equivalent to

```
DO I = 1 TO 5;
    DO J = 1 TO 10;
        Y(J,I) = SQRT(Z(J,I));
        END;
    END;
```

This is a particular case of array assignment. The rules of array assignment are summarized in Chapter C2.

The built-in array functions expect an array as an argument, and return a single (scalar) value. For example, HBOUND(X,N) gives the upper bound of the Nth dimension of the array X. Thus, the two statements

```
DECLARE (Z(3:10,-4:18),D) FIXED DECIMAL;
    D = HBOUND(Z,2);
```

set D to the number 18, the upper bound of the second dimension of Z.

P7 PROCEDURES

The built-in string functions operate on character strings. These will be discussed in Chapter P9.

The remainder of this chapter discusses user written procedures in PL/I. They are written in a manner very similar to that used in the text.

P7.1 Subroutines

PL/I subroutines begin with the statement

```
<name>: PROCEDURE (<parameter list>);
```

where <name> is any PL/I name consisting of seven or fewer characters, and <parameter list> is a list of dummy variables separated by commas. It is terminated with an END statement which may be followed by the name of the procedure being ended. (It is a good idea to include the name because the keyword END is used for so many different language constructs in PL/I.) The RETURN statement is identical to the return discussed in the text. Program P7.2 is a PL/I version of Program P7.2 to find the smallest and largest elements of an array. Note that the array A is declared by A(*). This indicates that it has one dimension, and that the size of the dimension will be determined at the time the subroutine is called. We do not have to state the actual size of the dimension inside the subroutine. It must be given, however, for the actual parameter value passed in from the calling procedure. The compiler does not have to allocate space for arrays which are parameters because the subroutine uses the space allocated to the actual parameter value. For example, if EXTREME is called from a procedure which includes the statements

```
DECLARE Q(0:100) FLOAT DECIMAL;
   ...
   CALL EXTREME(Q,50,S,B);
```

the array Q has 101 memory cells allocated for storing Q(0) to Q(100). EXTREME accesses cells Q(1) to Q(50) when it refers to A(1) to A(50).

Program P7.2 Subroutine to Find the Smallest and Largest Array Elements

```
EXTREME: PROCEDURE (A, N, SMALL, LARGE);
    /*  SMALL AND LARGE ARE SET TO THE SMALLEST AND LARGEST */
    /*  OF THE N ELEMENT ARRAY A IF N > 0.                  */
    /*  IF N <=0, SMALL <- 1E0 AND LARGE <- -1E0            */

    DECLARE (I, N) FIXED DECIMAL,
        (A(*), SMALL, LARGE) FLOAT DECIMAL;
    IF N <= 0
        THEN DO;  SMALL = 1E0; LARGE = -1E0; END;
        ELSE DO;
            SMALL = A(1);
            LARGE = A(1);
            I = 2;
            DO WHILE (I <= N);
                IF SMALL > A(I) THEN SMALL = A(I); ELSE;
                IF LARGE < A(I) THEN LARGE = A(I); ELSE;
                I = I + 1;
                END;
            END;
        RETURN;
    END EXTREME;
```

P7.1 Subroutines

The actual parameter values (arguments) passed to a subroutine must be of the right form. For example, the first argument in the subroutine EXTREME defined in program P7.2 must be an array. When a subroutine is called, it is informed where the arguments are stored in memory. When the subroutine accesses these parameters, it will expect to find data of the right type; if it has been told that the second parameter is FIXED DECIMAL, it expects to find a FIXED DECIMAL value. If the user passes a FLOAT DECIMAL value in the second position, the internal form will be used with disastrous results because the internal form of, say, 1 is nothing like the internal form of 1.E0. PL/I allows the user to tell the calling procedure what type of parameters are to be passed. For example, if we call EXTREME from a procedure containing

```
DECLARE Q(100) FIXED DECIMAL,
        (B, S) FLOAT DECIMAL,
        EXTREME ENTRY ( (*) FLOAT DECIMAL,
             FIXED DECIMAL, FLOAT DECIMAL,FLOAT DECIMAL),
   ...
   CALL EXTREME (Q, 50.0E0, B, S);
```

the subroutine accomplishes the desired effect, although the first two parameters are of the wrong type. Q is fixed, but the subroutine expects a FLOAT array. The declaration of EXTREME as an ENTRY followed by a list of argument types tells the compiler that EXTREME is a procedure which must be called with the declared parameter types. For example, the first parameter is declared to be (*) FLOAT DECIMAL. This says that it is a one-dimensional array of type FLOAT DECIMAL. When the array Q, which is of type FIXED DECIMAL, is passed, the compiler generates code to convert the type. (Note, however, that it is better to pass the correct type, as type conversions take computer time.) Similarly, the 50.0E0 is converted to a FIXED DECIMAL value. It is essential that the output parameters SMALL and LARGE have corresponding arguments of the same type, so B and S must be FLOAT DECIMAL.

Any variables declared inside the subroutine are totally local to that subroutine. For example, the variable I is used in EXTREME. It occupies a different place in memory from any variable named I used in the calling procedure, so that the person using EXTREME does not have to be aware of the variable names used internally in a subprocedure.

In PL/I, subroutines can be internal or external to the main program. We will not discuss external procedures here. By an internal procedure, we mean one that is defined within the main program. Program P7.2a indicates the way in which EXTREME is defined within the main procedure. Note that its definition appears between the main PROCEDURE statement and the END statement terminating the main procedure. Although the definition

Program P7.2a An Internal Procedure Definition

```
EXAMPLE: PROCEDURE OPTIONS(MAIN);
         ...
         CALL EXTREME(...)
         ...
         PUT LIST (...);
     EXTREME: PROCEDURE (A, N, SMALL, LARGE);
          declarations for EXTREME;
              statements defining extreme;
              RETURN;
         END EXTREME;
     END EXAMPLE;
```

of EXTREME appears (or can appear) immediately after an executable statement in the main program, EXTREME is executed only when it is called. Immediately after the statement preceding the definition of extreme (PUT LIST) is executed in Program P7.2a, the statement following the definition of EXTREME is executed; in this example it is END EXAMPLE. This terminates the execution of the main program.

If the user defines several subroutines, each can be included inside the main procedure, for example:

```
EX2: PROCEDURE OPTIONS(MAIN);
    declarations and body of main;
    SUB1: PROCEDURE (...);
        declarations and body of SUB1;
        END SUB1;
    SUB2: PROCEDURE (...);
        declarations and body of SUB2;
        END SUB2;
        ...
    END EX2;
```

Again, we emphasize that any variables declared inside the inner procedures are not known to the main procedure, or to the other subprocedures. In this way, each subprocedure has its own private storage. However, the names of the subprocedures are known, both to the main procedure and to the subprocedures. Thus, in the example above, SUB1 can be called from the main procedure or from any of the subprocedures, such as SUB2, that are declared within the main procedure. (Note that if the name SUB2 is used as a variable name inside SUB1, then the procedure SUB2 <u>cannot</u> be called from within SUB1, because inside SUB1 the name SUB2 is taken to be a variable name.)

We have just seen that PL/I subprocedures can be declared within the main procedure. They may also be declared within other subprocedures. Thus, the example above can be changed to

```
EX2: PROCEDURE OPTIONS(MAIN);
    declarations and body of main;
    SUB1: PROCEDURE (...);
        declarations and body if SUB1;
        SUB2: PROCEDURE (...);
            declarations and body of SUB2;
            END SUB2;
        END SUB1;
    ...
    END EX2;
```

In this case, SUB2 is declared within SUB1 because it appears between the PROCEDURE and END statements surrounding SUB1. Consequently, SUB2 is known to SUB1, but it is now known outside of SUB1 because <u>it is treated the same as variables declared within SUB1</u>. We will have further comments on the <u>nesting</u> of subprocedures in Chapter P9.

P7.2 Function Subprograms

PL/I function subprograms are defined in the same way as subroutines, except that they must specify the value to be returned. This is done as in our informal language by specifying the value in parentheses following a RETURN statement. For example, RETURN(17.EO*A) returns the value of the expression 17.0*A as the value of the function. The type of the value returned should be specified in the PROCEDURE declaration statement. This is illustrated in Program P7.3 which defines the function DRAG used as an illustration in the text. The first statement, DRAG: PROCEDURE (X) RETURNS(FLOAT DECIMAL); tells the compiler that the procedure DRAG has a single parameter, X, and has a FLOAT DECIMAL value. In this example, the body of the definition consists of a single RETURN statement only. A function definition can consist of any valid section of code, and can declare any additional internal variables it needs.

Program P7.3 A PL/I Function Definition

```
DRAG: PROCEDURE (X) RETURNS (FLOAT DECIMAL);
    DECLARE X FLOAT DECIMAL;
        RETURN (.32E-2*X**3 + .1364E0*X);
    END DRAG;
```

Program P7.3a shows a complete PL/C job that prints a table of the values of DRAG for arguments between 1 and 20. Note that DRAG is also declared in the containing program to be an ENTRY, as EXTREME was in Program P7.2a. In this case, however, we must also state that the value returned by DRAG is FLOAT DECIMAL.

Program P7.3a Complete PL/C Job with the Function DRAG

```
        $PL/C
         TABLE: PROCEDURE OPTIONS (MAIN);
                DECLARE I FIXED DECIMAL,
                        DRAG ENTRY (FLOAT DECIMAL) RETURNS (FLOAT DECIMAL);
                    PUT PAGE LIST ('X','DRAG(X)','X','DRAG(X)');
                    DO I = 1 TO 10;
                        PUT SKIP LIST (I,DRAG(I),I+10,DRAG(I+10));
                        END;
             DRAG: PROCEDURE (X) RETURNS (FLOAT DECIMAL);
                    DECLARE X FLOAT DECIMAL;
                    RETURN (.32E-2*X**3 + .1364E0*X);
                    END DRAG;
             END TABLE;
$DATA
$STOP
```

A PL/I subprocedure may have as many parameters as desired. The actual parameter values to a function must satisfy the same criteria as the actual parameter values to a subroutine, that is, if the dummy parameter is an array, the actual parameter value must also be an array of the same dimension. A function should always be declared as an ENTRY in the calling procedure so that the the compiler can arrange for argument conversion if necessary.

Problems

1. Write a subroutine that copies the N element array B to the N element array C.

2. Write a subroutine that adds two N element vectors A and B together, leaving the result in the N element vector C. (That is, C(I) = A(I) + B(I) for I from 1 to N.)

3. Write a subroutine that calculates the roots of a quadratic equation A*X**2 + B*X + C = 0, and returns their values in R1 and R2 if the roots are real, or returns the real part in R1 and the imaginary part in R2 if the roots are imaginary. A, B, C, R1, R2, and I should be parameters, and I should be set to +1 if the roots are real, -1 otherwise.

4. Write a function whose value is the fourth root of its floating-point argument. (Use the built-in function SQRT.)

5. Write a function TANGNT(X) whose value is the tangent of x, which is defined as sin(x)/cos(x). Use any of the built-in functions except for TAN(X).

6. Write a function whose value is the index of the smallest element in an N element array A, or zero if N is less than one. N and A should be parameters.

7. Write a function whose parameters are an N element array B, N, and X. The value of the function should be an integer K such that X = B(K) if such a K exists between 1 and N, otherwise, it should be zero.

Programs in text to convert to PL/I: P7.5 and P7.6.

Problems in text to do in PL/I: 6, 7, 8, and 9.

P8 CONTROL REVISITED

This chapter covers the PL/I counting loops and other aspects of the DO statement. It also discusses use of IF and ON statements to achieve reasonable program structure.

P8.1 PL/I DO Loops

The PL/I counting loop is introduced with the keyword DO, as used in the example below:

```
DO K = 2 TO 10;
    body of loop
    END;
```

This causes the body of the loop to be executed with K taking on the values 2, 3, 4, ..., 10 in order. The *range* of the DO is indicated by its matching END statement. It is often a good idea to label these to avoid confusion. If a label is placed in front of the DO, the same label may be placed after the END, for example

```
OUTER: DO K = 5 TO 50;
    body of loop
    END OUTER;
```

The form of the counting DO statement itself is

```
DO <var> = <exp1> TO <exp2> BY <exp3>;
```

where <var> is the controlled variable which is to be incremented after each pass though the loop, <exp1> is an expression whose value is assigned to <var> initially, <exp3> is the increment, and <exp2> is the final value. The increment can be negative, in which case <var> is decremented until it goes below the final value. The increment <exp3> does not have to be specified, in which case it is taken as one. For example, DO K = 3.1 TO 6.9 assigns the values 3.1, 4.1, 5.1, and 6.1 to K on four successive passes through the loop, assuming that K is declared to be a variable type that can store values like 3.1. (If K is an integer, it will take the values 3, 4, 5, and 6 in this example.)

Recall that the DO statement is also used without the counting indication and without a WHILE clause to form a compound statement. Therefore, be careful not to be confused by these different uses of DO in a program. The two uses are illustrated in Program *P8.1* which is a PL/I transliteration of Program P8.1.

The expressions used to form the initial values, increments, and end values for counting loops can take any form. They are evaluated before the loop is executed for the first time, and are *not* re-evaluated after each pass through the loop. Thus, the loop

```
J = 2;
DO I = 1 TO 11 BY J;
    J = J + 1;
    END;
```

is executed six times with I equal to 1, 3, 5, 7, 9, and 11, even though J is changed inside the loop, and finishes with a value of 8.

Good programming practice indicates that the controlled variable should not be changed inside the controlling loop, although PL/I does not forbid it. A program that does change the controlled variable is much harder to understand--how would you like to

Program P8.1 Find the Maximum Element of an Array

```
MAXIMUM: PROCEDURE (A, N) RETURNS (FIXED DECIMAL);

    /*  COMPUTE THE MAXIMUM OF THE ELEMENTS IN A(I)  */
    /*  I = 1 TO N, AND SET THE INDEX OF THE LARGEST */
    /*  AS THE VALUE OF THE FUNCTION.                */

    DECLARE (A(*), N, I, J, BIG) FIXED DECIMAL;
        IF N <= 0
            THEN J = 0;
            ELSE DO;
                J   = 1;
                BIG = A(1);
                SEARCH_LOOP: DO I = 2 TO N;
                    IF BIG < A(I)
                        THEN DO;
                            J = I;
                            BIG = A(I);
                            END;
                        ELSE;
                    END SEARCH_LOOP;
            END;
        RETURN (J);
    END MAXIMUM;
```

try and decipher a program containing the following sequence?

```
DO I = 1 TO N;
    I = 2*I;
    ...
    END;
```

Programs P8.2 and P8.3 introduce the idea of a loop which can be terminated either by the count running out or by the failure of a condition. PL/I does this in a manner similar to the text, using the statement

```
DO var = exp1 TO exp2 BY exp3 WHILE (condition);
```

The use of this statement is shown in Program P8.2 which is a PL/I version of the corresponding program in the text. Note that the value of the controlled variable I is

Program P8.2 Search for an Value in an Array

```
SEARCH: PROCEDURE (B, N, X) RETURNS (FIXED DECIMAL);

    /*  SEARCH IS 0 IF X IS NOT IN ARRAY B, OTHERWISE   */
    /*  SEARCH IS THE INDEX OF THE FIRST ELEMENT IN THE */
    /*  N ELEMENT ARRAY B EQUAL TO X.                   */

    DECLARE (B(*), X) FLOAT DECIMAL,
            (N, I) FIXED DECIMAL;
         DO I = 1 TO N WHILE (X ¬= B(I));
             END;
         IF I = N + 1 THEN I = 0; ELSE;
         RETURN (I);
     END SEARCH;
```

known when the loop terminates; it has the first value that exceeded the range of values specified by the TO expression, in this case, N+1, or an I such that B(I) = X.

P8.2 Implementing Case Statements in PL/I

Since PL/I does not have a case statement, its effect must be simulated using other statements. The most direct way is to write a series of separate IF statements. For example, *case* (1,2,3,4) *of* N could be simulated by writing

```
/*  CASE (1,2,3,4) OF N */
    IF N = 1 THEN ...; ELSE;
    IF N = 2 THEN ...; ELSE;
    IF N = 3 THEN ...; ELSE;
    IF N = 4 THEN ...; ELSE;
    /* OTHER */
    IF N < 1 ¦ N > 4 THEN ...; ELSE;
    /* END CASE */
```

(We will see in the next chapter that the condition N < 1 ¦ N > 4 is true if N is less than 1 or greater than 4.) Unfortunately, this is a slow way to do it because all five IF statements are executed each time the case construct is executed. An alternative is to use PL/I LABEL variables and constants. These should be used sparingly, because they can lead to hard to follow programs, but they are of value in case statement simulation. PL/I allows us to declare a variable as a LABEL. In this example, we will declare an array of four items as LABELs, by writing

```
DECLARE CASE(4) LABEL;
```

in the declarations at the start of the procedure or block containing the case statement. Now we will translate the case statement into

```
/* CASE (1,2,3,4) OF N */
    IF N < 1 ¦ N > 4 THEN GO TO OTHER_CASE; ELSE;
    GO TO CASE(N);
    CASE(1): ...; GO TO DONE_CASE;
    CASE(2): ...; GO TO DONE_CASE;
    CASE(3): ...; GO TO DONE_CASE;
    CASE(4): ...; GO TO DONE_CASE;
    OTHER_CASE: ...;
DONE_CASE: ;
```

The GO TO CASE(N); statement will only be executed if N is between 1 and 4. Consequently, the GO TO branches to one of the four LABELs CASE(1) through CASE(4). These are defined by their appearance in front of statements corresponding to the appropriate cases to be executed. If N is not between 1 and 4, the statements following OTHER_CASE are executed. In all cases, execution finishes up at the label DONE_CASE.

P8.3 The ON Statement

The PL/I ON statement is a control statement that is used to specify the action to be taken when unusual conditions arise, such as end of file, overflow, or subscripts that are out of range. The form of the statement is

```
            ON condition On-unit
or          ON condition SYSTEM
```

For example, the statement ON ENDFILE(SYSIN) GO TO LOOP_END tells the computer that if an end of file occurs on the unit SYSIN (the standard input unit), the statement GO TO LOOP_END is to be executed. The condition following the ON keyword describes a condition that may occur in the future. Execution of the ON statement does not cause the On-unit (in this example, the GO TO LOOP_END) to be executed, it tells the computer what is to be done if the condition occurs. If an ON statement has not been executed for a condition, such as end of file, the "standard system action" will be taken. In most cases, this means that program execution is terminated, so the ON statement provides a mechanism by which the programmer can keep control when such a condition occurs.

Once an ON statement has been executed for a condition, the computer executes the action specified in the ON-unit whenever the condition arises. If the programmer wishes to change the action to be taken, another ON statement must be executed. The action specified in the subsequent ON statement will supercede the action specified in the previous ON statement. For example, if a program is to read in a set of positive data followed by an optional set of negative data, it could be structured as follows:

```
ON ENDFILE(SYSIN) GO TO LP1;
Loop to read data, terminating on negative value.
LP1:
IF last data value read negative
    THEN DO;
        ON ENDFILE(SYSIN) GO TO LP2;
        Loop to read data, terminating on positive value.
        END;
    ELSE;
LP2:
```

If the data contains positive values followed by negative values followed by another positive value, neither GO TO is ever executed. If the data consists of positive values followed by negative values with no more positive values, the GO TO LP2 is executed when an attempt to read beyond the end of file in the second loop occurs. If the programmer wishes the standard system action to occur, the second form of the ON statement should be executed, namely, ON ENDFILE(SYSIN) SYSTEM.

In the example above, we have used a GO TO as the On-unit. The On-unit can take other forms; it can consist of an assignment statement or a BEGIN block described in the next chapter, for example. If an assignment statement appears as an On-unit, the statement is executed when the condition arises, then processing continues from the point at which it was stopped by the condition. If, for example, the condition is ENDFILE, we could assign values to the variables which could not be read and continue. In most cases, you will find that the GO TO statement is the most suitable component for an On-unit.

The On-unit may refer to variables or program labels. Clearly, these must be "known" to the computer at the time the On-unit is executed. For example, suppose that an ON statement is executed inside a subprocedure, and that this statement contains a reference to a variable or label defined within the subprocedure. At the time the condition arises, that variable or label must be part of the program that is currently executing. If a return has already been made from the subprocedure, the variable or label has effectively disappeared. Consequently, when an ON statement is executed inside a subprocedure, it is only "active" as long as the subprocedure is "active." Once a RETURN is executed, the On-unit specified by the ON statement "disappears." Thus, at LABEL X2 in the code below, an end of file will cause a GO TO L2 to be executed, but at the label X1 or X3, an end of file will cause a GO TO L1 to be executed, even though, at the label X3 the ON ... GO TO L2 has already been executed.

```
     ON ENDFILE(SYSIN) GO TO L1;
X1:  ...
     CALL PROC1;
X3:  ...
     PROC1: PROCEDURE;
        ...
        ON ENDFILE(SYSIN) GO TO L2;
  X2:   ...
        RETURN
        END PROC1;
 END;
```

Thus, each procedure that is active can have an On-unit associated with each condition. When a procedure is called, the On-unit is the currently specified action; it can be changed by executing an ON statement. The effect of that ON statement is lost when a return is made from the procedure. The same effect occurs when BEGIN blocks (discussed in the next chapter) are entered and left.

Problems

1. How many times does each of the following DO statements cause a loop to be executed?

   a. DO I = 10 TO 50 BY 2;
   b. DO J = 1 TO 100 BY 50;
   c. DO K = 27 TO 81 BY 3;
   d. DO L = 63 TO 33 BY 30;

2. Which of the following are valid PL/I statements?

   a. DO WHILE A > B;
   b. DO I = 1 TO 10 BY -1;
   c. DO FOR I = 5 TO 10;
   d. DO I = 1 TO 100 WHILE (I < 50);
   e. DO I = 10 TO 1;

3. Write a DO loop to reverse the order of the N element array B(I).

4. Write nested DO loops to form the sum of all elements of the N by N array B(I,J) for which I is greater than J.

5. Repeat problem 4, this time summing only those elements for which B(I,J) is positive.

6. Consider the PL/I statement

```
PUT SKIP EDIT ('*', I = 1 TO N) (100A(1));
```

If N is between 1 and 100, this will print a line containing N consecutive asterisk characters. Use this technique to print a bar graph of the elements of the array B(K), K = 1 to N. For example, if N is 3, and B(1) to B(3) contain 3.2, 6.7, and 4.8, then the graph should look like

```
1 ***
2 *******
3 *****
```

Programs in Chapter P8 to convert to PL/I: P8.4, P8.5

Problems in the text to do in PL/I: 3, 4, 5, 6, 7, and 8.

P9 DATA REVISITED

PL/I handles several types of data besides the arithmetic types we have been discussing. It can work with character strings, strings of bits (zero or one digits) which function as groups of logical variables, and variables, called pointers, which indicate where other data can be found in memory. (Pointers are not available in PL/C, so will be mentioned only briefly here.) PL/I also allows a much more flexible naming system for groups of variables called structures. These allow a natural hierachical naming to be used for groups of data items which concern a single entity.

PL/I allows for more arithmetic types than we have discussed so far. The first section discusses these additional arithmetic types.

P9.1 Precision and Complex Attributes

So far we have mentioned FIXED and FLOAT data, either of which can be represented in DECIMAL or BINARY internally. PL/I arithmetic data has four _type attributes_ which indicate how it is represented internally. The first type attribute is called the _scale_ attribute. It indicates whether the data is stored in FIXED or FLOAT form. The second type attribute is the _base_ attribute which indicates whether it is represented in BINARY or DECIMAL. The third type attribute is the _precision_ attribute, which indicates how many digits are used to store the data (or the mantissa of the data in the case of a floating-point number). So far, we have never specified the precision. In that case, PL/I uses a _default_ precision, which is implementation dependent. In IBM systems, the default precisions are:

```
FIXED DECIMAL - 5 digits        FLOAT DECIMAL - 6 digits
FIXED BINARY  - 15 bits         FLOAT BINARY  - 21 bits
```

These precisions are determined by the number of bits in a word on the IBM 370 computers for which the implementation is written. However, it is possible to use other precisions. Internally, the computer can store a single number in several words, or can pack more than one number of few digits into a single word. The PL/I programmer does not have to be concerned about the way this is done beause PL/I allows the user to specify the precision of the variables used up to the maximum precision available. The compiler takes care of assigning the appropriate number of storage cells to store the data.

The precision of floating-point data can be specified in the declaration of variables by writing the number of digits after the type attribute. For example,

```
DECLARE (A,B) FLOAT DECIMAL(9), Z FLOAT BINARY (46);
```

declares A and B to be floating-point variables with _at least_ 9 decimal digits of precision in the mantissa, and Z to be a floating-point variable with _at least_ 46 bits of precision in the mantissa. We say _at least_, because PL/I uses the most convenient internal representation available in the computer. For IBM 370 computers, this means that single precision is used for up to 6 decimal or 21 binary floating-point numbers, and double precision is used for up to 16 decimal or 53 binary digits. Larger precisions are not possible, and therefore disallowed in IBM implementations of PL/I. Note that because the most convenient representation is used, a change of precision may not change the numerical results because the same representation may be used.

The precision of FIXED data can be specified in a similar manner. For example

```
DECLARE I FIXED DECIMAL(8), (K,L) FIXED BINARY(27);
```

declares I to contain 8 decimal digits, and K and L to contain 27 bits each. I, K, and L are integers with this declaration. The maximum precision allowed is 15 decimal digits, or 31 bits respectively.

In PL/I, FIXED data is not restricted to being integral. For example, values such as 34.25, representing, say, a dollar value, are fixed-point values with two digits after the decimal point. In PL/I, variables can be declared to have this form by specifying the precision and the number of digits after the point. For example,

```
DECLARE (P, Q) FIXED DECIMAL(7,2);
```

declares P and Q to be variables storing seven-digit numbers with two digits after the decimal point. After such a declaration, we can write

```
Q = 4;
P = 53.21 * Q;
PUT LIST (P);
```

and get the result printed as 212.84. The constants in the first statement are fixed decimal numbers--53.21 has precision (4,2) because it has four digits in all with two after the decimal point, and 4 is a precision (1,0) number.

In scientific programming, we generally do not specify the precision unless it is to force the use of double precision floating point. Precision specification is more important in data processing work using fixed point. However, if the programmer is planning to do much arithmetic in fixed point, the IBM reference manual should be consulted for all of the rules which govern the precision of results. Occasionally it is possible to get overflow in situations which do not seem unreasonable until the rules are understood.

The final type attribute for arithmetic data is <u>mode</u>, namely, REAL or COMPLEX. REAL is the default attribute of all arithmetic data. COMPLEX must be declared. For example,

```
DECLARE Q FLOAT COMPLEX DECIMAL(16);
```

declares Q to be a complex variable whose real and imaginary parts are each represented as FLOAT DECIMAL(16) values. (The order of the type keywords is not important. We could have written COMPLEX FLOAT DECIMAL(16), for example.)

Complex constants can be formed in two ways. A number can be written as the sum of real and imaginary parts in which the imaginary part is followed by the character I. For example, 2.5E0 + 4.1E1I is the complex number whose real part has value 2.5 and imaginary part has value 41. Alternatively, one can write COMPLEX(2.5, 41). This uses the built-in function COMPLEX which can also be used with real expressions as parameters. (See Section <u>C3</u>.) For example, the following section of code computes the two roots of the quadratic equation A*X**2 + B*X + C = 0: where A, B, and C are REAL, but we have allowed for complex roots.

```
DECLARE ((R1,R2) COMPLEX, A, B, C) FLOAT DECIMAL;
    ... code to set values of A, B, and C
    R1 = (-B + SQRT(COMPLEX(B**2 - 4.0E0*A*C, 0.E0)))/(2.0E0*A);
    R2 = C/(R1*A);
```

(Note that attributes can be "factored" to save writing. The attributes FLOAT DECIMAL apply to everything inside the outer parentheses, while COMPLEX applies only to R1 and R2.) The function COMPLEX had to be used in the calculation of R1 to force the argument of SQRT to be complex. This causes SQRT to return a complex result which will have a zero imaginary part if the argument is positive real. The second root is calculated from the fact that the product of the two roots is C/A.

COMPLEX numbers can be input and output using the GET and PUT statements. In list-directed input and output, a complex value is a pair of reals externally. The second item is followed by the character I, and the real and imaginary parts are separated with a plus or minus sign. No space or comma may appear between the real and complex parts. In edit-directed I/O, a complex value is described by a pair of real format items enclosed in parentheses and preceded by the character C. For example, a format description C((F10,3),(F10,3)) describes a complex value which is to appear as a pair of fixed-point values occupying 10 columns each with three digits after their decimal points. The data input should not include the character I, and no I appears in the output.

P9.2 Character Strings

PL/I character strings are declared with the attribute CHARACTER (which can be abbreviated to CHAR), followed by the length of the string. Thus,

```
DCL (A, B, W(12)) CHARACTER(15), Q CHAR (5);
```

declares A, B, and the twelve element vector W each to be 15-character strings, and the variable Q to be a 5-character string. Character string constants are character strings surrounded by single quotes, as in the text. Assignment of character strings causes the string on the right-hand side of the assignment to be truncated or padded with blanks on the right as necessary to get the appropriate length. These operations are exactly the same as described in the text. The same is true for comparison of strings. PL/I allows any of the relational operators to be used to compare strings. The collating sequence in given under Character-String Operators in Chapter C1. The use of comparisons is illustrated in program P9.1, which is a PL/I version of Program P9.1.

Program P9.1 Character String Search in PL/I

```
PRNT_SC: PROCEDURE (STUDENT, SCORE, N, NAME);

    /*  SEARCH ARRAY STUDENT OF NAMES FOR ENTRY              */
    /*  EQUAL TO NAME.  IF SUCH ENTRY FOUND, PRINT            */
    /*  CORRESPONDING ENTRY IN SCORE.                         */

    DCL (N, I, K, SCORE(*)) FIXED DECIMAL,
        (STUDENT(*), NAME) CHARACTER(*);
        K = 0;
        /*    SET K TO INDEX OF NAME IN STUDENT  */
        DO I = 1 TO N WHILE (K = 0);
            IF STUDENT(I) >= NAME THEN K = I; ELSE;
            END;
        IF K ¬= 0
            THEN
                IF NAME = STUDENT(K)
                    THEN PUT SKIP LIST
                           ('SCORE OF', NAME, 'IS', SCORE(K));
                    ELSE PUT SKIP LIST ('NO RECORD OF', NAME);
            ELSE PUT SKIP LIST ('NO RECORD OF', NAME);
        RETURN;
    END PRNT_SC;
```

Strings can be input and output with any of the I/O statements. List-directed output causes the string to be printed without quotes, while list-directed input reads a string surrounded by quotes. Edit-directed I/O uses the format descriptor A to describe character strings. For example, to read a 10-character string from the first ten columns of the next line into variable B we can write

```
GET SKIP EDIT (B) (A(10));
```

If B has been declared as CHAR(14), the ten input characters are padded to fourteen by appending 4 blanks on the right. In edit-directed output, the format descriptor need not have a length specified, in which case the length of the character string in the output list is used. For example, if B is a 14-character string,

```
PUT SKIP LIST (B) (A);
```

outputs 14 characters on the start of the next line.

The maximum length string allowed in PL/I is 256 characters. In addition to fixed length strings, PL/I allows strings to have variable length. However, the maximum length must still be declared. For example

```
DECLARE (P, Q) CHARACTER(80) VARYING;
```

declares P and Q to be varying length character strings whose maximum length is 80. Initially they have a length of zero--that is, they are <u>null</u> strings. When a string is assigned to a VARYING string, the length is set to the length of the string on the right-hand side provided that it is no longer than the maximum length permitted. If it is too long, truncation on the right to the maximum length occurs.

<u>Character String Operations</u>

Concatenation is indicated by the character pair ¦¦. For example, 'ABC' ¦¦ 'DEFG' is the 7-character string 'ABCDEFG'. Consider the statement

```
Q = Q ¦¦ '123';
```

where Q is CHARACTER(5) VARYING. If this is the first assignment to Q, it results in Q being '123', a string of length three, since the initial value of Q is the null string. However, if this statement is repeated a second time, the result is '12312' because Q ¦¦ '123', which is '123123', is truncated to the maximum length of Q, namely five.

The other string operations are provided as built-in functions. The principal ones are

LENGTH(S)	- an integer equal to the length of string S
INDEX(S,S1)	- an integer equal to the position of the first character in S such that string S1 matches string S from that point for the length of S1. The result is zero if S1 not in S.
SUBSTR(S,I,J)	- the substring of length J starting at position I of string S. If J is omitted, the substring continues to the end of S.
VERIFY(S,S1)	- the index of the first character in S that does not match any of the characters in S1. The result is zero if all characters match.

P9.3 Bit Strings and Logical Variables

PL/I has a data type called BIT which is a string of bits. In many ways, a bit string is the same as a character string, so that the material in the previous section is applicable to bit strings. The only difference is that bit-string constants are written in the form 'string'B, where string is any string of zero and one characters up to a maximum of 256. Any of the string operations, including concatenation, comparison, and built-in functions can be applied to bit strings. They are declared using the attribute BIT, optionally modified by VARYING. For example,

```
DCL Q1 BIT(10), Q2 BIT(25) VARYING;
```

declares Q1 to be a bit string of 10 bits, and Q2 to be a varying length string with a maximum of 25 bits. The initial value of Q2 is the null string. Bit strings can be assigned to character strings, in which case they become strings of zero and one characters. If a character string is assigned to a bit string, the character string must be a string of zeros and ones.

The more important usage of bit strings is as sets of logical values, where each bit represent a single logical value, 0 for false and 1 for true. The conditional control statements test the value of bit strings. If the string is longer than one bit, the condition is true if any of the bits are one. The result of a comparison by a relational operator is a bit string of length one. Thus, the value of "5 > 3" is '1'B, and of "4 = 7.1" is '0'B. The logical operators, <u>and</u>, <u>or</u>, and <u>not</u>, are represented by the characters &, ¦, and ¬. These operators operate on bit strings and give a bit string as an answer. Most of the time, we use the logical operators on bit strings of length one, and think of them as working with the values true and false. Thus, "A > B ¦ C < D" is true if either A is greater than B or C is less than D. The precedence of these operators relative to each other is as given in the text.

If the logical operators are applied to strings of length greater than one, the operations are performed on the bit positions individually. For example, the logical <u>or</u> of two strings of length three is a string of length three whose ith bit is the logical <u>or</u> of the ith bits of the two operands. <u>And</u> and <u>or</u> are binary operations requiring two operands. If the operands are of unequal length, the shorter is extended with zeros to give it the length of the latter.

BIT strings can be input and output in a way similar to character strings. In list-directed I/O, the string should be input in the same form as a constant. In edit-directed I/O, the field descriptor is B(w) for a w-column field of bits. On output, the descriptor B can be used, in which case the length is obtained from the data.

P9.4 Structures and Pointers

Frequently, we find ourselves working with groups of data items, all of which concern a single item. For example, we may have a list of information concerning each employee in a company. A record for a single employee might contain NAME, WAGE_RATE, ADDRESS, TAX_INFORMATION, AGE, and DEPT_NUMBER. A program referring to this would obviously be clearer and more concise if it could refer to the group of names as a unit in, for example, input/output statements. PL/I allows this, and permits statements such as

```
PUT SKIP LIST (EMPLOYEE);
```

where employee has been defined to be the collection of data above. The collection is defined when the variables are declared by using a <u>structure</u>. The declaration

```
DECLARE 1 EMPLOYEE,
      2 NAME CHAR(20),
      2 WAGE_RATE FIXED DECIMAL (7,2),
      2 ADDRESS CHAR (40),
```

declares the identifier EMPLOYEE to refer to a set of three data items, NAME, WAGE_RATE, and ADDRESS. A reference to EMPLOYEE is a reference to all three data items. EMPLOYEE is a level one name. It does not have a data type explicitly declared, because it is a structure. The data items making up that structure do have a data type however, in this case, FIXED and CHARACTER. The statement PUT ... (EMPLOYEE); is exactly the same as the statement PUT ...(NAME, WAGE_RATE, ADDRESS);.

A structure can have several levels. The example above has only two, but we might want to add more information such as TAX_INFORMATION, where TAX_INFORMATION is itself structured. For example,

```
DCL 1 EMPLOYEE(100),
        2 NAME CHAR(20),
        2 WAGE_RATE FIXED DECIMAL (7,2),
        2 ADDRESS CHAR(20),
        2 TAX_INFORMATION,
            3 TOTAL_TAXES FIXED DECIMAL (10,2),
            3 WAGES_TO_DATE FIXED DECIMAL (11,2),
            3 NUMBER_DEPENDENTS FIXED(2),
        2 DEPT CHAR(5);
```

This statement declares EMPLOYEE to be an array of 100 structures, each with identical format. Each has five second level names: four are data items, the fifth is a substructure. The programmer can now refer to EMPLOYEE(I), and it is the same as referring to the seven variables NAME(I), WAGE_RATE(I), ADDRESS(I), TOTAL_TAXES(I), WAGES_TO_DATE(I), NUMBER_DEPENDENTS(I), and DEPT(I). Alternatively, a single one of the data items can be referenced by using its name. In this example, a reference can also be made to TAX_INFORMATION(I) to access the three data items in that substructure.

In many cases, we will want to use the names of individual data items in several different structures. For example, we might want to define an array EMPLOYEE as above, and another structure NEW_EMPLOYEE with the same structure. (This could be done by changing the first line of the declaration above to DECLARE (1 EMPLOYEE(100), 1 NEW_EMPLOYEE),.) Both structures would contain the identifiers ADDRESS, etc., so a reference to ADDRESS would not be unique. In this case, a _qualified name_ must be used. This takes the form EMPLOYEE.ADDRESS or NEW_EMPLOYEE.ADDRESS. This means that the identifier ADDRESS should be sought in the structures EMPLOYEE or NEW_EMPLOYEE respectively. If the structures have been given the same form, the assignment statement

```
EMPLOYEE(I) = NEW_EMPLOYEE;
```

assigns each data item in NEW_EMPLOYEE to each in EMPLOYEE(I), a much more concise description of the operation that a list of individual assignment statements.

Pointers

PL/C does not have a specific data type for pointers, so array indices must be used as described in the text. Some examples are given in Chapter A4. However, PL/I has a data type called POINTER (abbreviated PTR) which defines a variable whose value is the "location" of another variable. The use of pointer variables requires an understanding of some of the storage management facilities in PL/I, so we will restrict ourselves to a few very general remarks here. PL/I permits the user to control the allocation of storage to dynamically changing collections of data. (The chained lists discussed in Chapter A4 are examples of such dynamically changing collections. The number of items in a list can change during execution.) In PL/I, this is specified by declaring variables in a suitable manner, and allocating space to the variable. For example,

```
DECLARE X FLOAT BINARY BASED (Q);
```

declares variable X to contain a floating-point value. However, it does not allocate storage to X. That is done in an ALLOCATE statement. The statement "ALLOCATE X" allocates storage to X and cause the variable Q to point to it. A second execution of "ALLOCATE X" causes additional storage to be allocated to a new generation of X. If we wanted to continue to refer to the old generation of X, we could keep a copy of a pointer to X. If, for example, we executed the following code:

```
DCL X FLOAT BINARY BASED (P),
    Q POINTER;
    ALLOCATE X;
    Q = P;
    ALLOCATE X;
```

we can refer to the latest generation of X as X or P -> X. The first generation of X is referenced by Q -> X. The symbol -> means "pointing at", so Q -> X means the version of X pointed at by Q. Since Q was assigned the value of P after the first generation of X was allocated, it contains a pointer to that generation.

P9.5 Initial Values

In PL/I, INITIAL is an attribute that can be specified for variables at the time of declaration. The keyword can be abbreviated to INIT. It appears along with the other attributes of data, and is followed by parentheses containing the initial value. For example,

```
DCL X FLOAT DECIMAL INITIAL (5.3E0);
```

declares X and gives it the initial value 0.53E1. This value is given to X when space is allocated to X. If several variables have been grouped, the initial values can also be grouped. For example

```
DCL ((A, B) FIXED, C FLOAT) DECIMAL INIT (15, -5, 2.5E0),
    D CHARACTER(10) INIT ('1234567');
```

declares A, B, C, and D, and initializes them to contain 15, -5, 0.25E0, and '1234567b̸b̸b̸', respectively. The initial values of an array are assigned in row order. If insufficient values are specified, the remaining elements of an array, or any other variables, are not initialized. Repetition factors can be used to repeat the same initial value or group of initial values. For example

```
DCL A(10,5) INITIAL ( (20)0.0E0, (5)(1.0E0, 0.0E0) );
```

declares the first 20 elements (4 rows) of A to be initialized to zero, and the next ten elements to be set to floating point 1, 0, 1, 0, 1, 0, 1, 0, 1, and 0 respectively. The last 20 elements are not initialized by this statement.

Problems

1. Write a program to "code" a piece of text by replacing each of the letters with another letter according to a table which should be the first part of the input. For example,

B might be replaced by Z and C with Q, etc. Use any non-alphabetic character you wish to terminate the input.

2. Write a "big letter" program which reads a card containing a series of words, and prints each word using "big" letters, such as

```
BBBBB        III       GGGG
B   B         I       G    G
B   B         I       G
BBBBB         I       G
B   B         I       G   GG
B   B         I       G    G
BBBBB        III       GGGG
```

Define each big letter using suitable INITIAL attributes.

3. Read a line containing three characters. The first and third should be T or F standing for _true_ or _false_. The middle one should be A or O standing for _and_ or _or_. Output a single character indicating the value of the three characters considered as a logical expression.

4. Input a line containing a sequence of the characters T, F, O, A, and N, standing for _true_, _false_, _or_, _and_, and _not_. If they form a valid logical expression, print the value of that expression, if not print an error message.

5. Program _P9.1_ has two copies of the statement PUT SKIP LIST ('NO RECORD OF',NAME); rewrite it using a logical operator to eliminate the second copy.

Problem in text to do in PL/I: 5.

P10 COMMUNICATION BETWEEN PROCEDURES

PL/I provides many of the features discussed in Chapter P10 of the text. Global storage between procedures is obtained by the nesting of procedures within other procedures. This is the principal topic of the Section P10.1. Global storage can also be obtained by the EXTERNAL attribute. This is also covered in the Section P10.1. Variables in PL/I are dynamic (called AUTOMATIC) unless declared otherwise. The STATIC and AUTOMATIC attributes are the topic of section P10.2. The BEGIN block also plays an important role in the allocation of storage; it too is discussed in Section P10.2. The following section covers the ENTRY statement which can be used to define additional entry points to a procedure. Finally, we will examine the mechanisms used for passing parameters in PL/I.

P10.1 Local Storage and EXTERNAL Variables

In PL/I, if a variable is declared inside a procedure (a practice followed exclusively in the text and so far in this manual), the variable is local to the procedure unless stated otherwise. However, we have seen that the definitions of PL/I procedures can be nested inside one another, that is, the definition of one procedure, from its initial PROCEDURE statement to its final END statement, can appear between the initial PROCEDURE statement and the final END statement of another procedure. When this is done, the name of the inner, or nested, procedure is known within the outer procedure, but not outside of that procedure. The basic rule is very simple--any identifier declared within a procedure is known within that procedure but not outside. Since the name of a procedure is an identifier as much as the name of a variable or a program label, the <u>scope</u> of knowledge of a procedure definition is confined to the procedure containing the definition.

This rule is followed very logically--any identifier declared within a procedure is known within that procedure, and hence is known within any procedure nested inside. For example, in the following definitions of procedures P and Q, the variables X and Y are known not only in procedure P, but also in procedure Q. However, the variable A in procedure Q is <u>not</u> the same as the variable A in procedure P because it is redeclared in procedure Q. The rule says that if it is declared in procedure Q it is known inside Q but not outside, and therefore is local to Q. Hence, variable A inside Q must be a different A from variable A outside of Q. The procedure Q is known inside P, but not outside of P, so if P is contained within an outer procedure (for example, the main procedure) Q would not be known in that outer procedure.

```
P: PROCEDURE (...);
   DCL (A, X, Y) FLOAT DECIMAL;
   ...
   Q: PROCEDURE (...);
      DCL A FIXED DECIMAL;
      ...
      END Q;
   ...
   END P;
```

The fact that variables can be referenced by name directly provides a very powerful mechanism for accessing data in related procedures. If, for example, in writing a subroutine to perform a complex task, we need to define a number of inner procedures to make the structure reasonable, it is not necessary to pass all variables from the outer procedure to inner procedures. Their definitions can be nested inside the outer procedure so they can access the data directly. This also has the advantage of "hiding" the names of the inner procedures from other users. This is illustrated in the following example:

```
SOLVE: PROCEDURE (A, B, N);
    DCL (A, B, N, V, X(N)) FIXED DECIMAL;
        ...
        CALL SUB1 (A);
        CALL SUB2 (4.5E6 - A);
        ...
    SUB1: PROCEDURE (R);
        DCL (R, A, V) FIXED DECIMAL;
        ...
        END SUB1;
    SUB2: PROCEDURE (S);
        DCL (S, A) FIXED DECIMAL;
        ...
        END SUB2;
    END SOLVE;
```

The scope of the identifiers in this section of code is as follows:

B and N	These are known throughout SOLVE, including SUB1 and SUB2 since they are declared inside SOLVE. They are parameters to SOLVE. Note that a reference to B or N in SUB1 is a reference to the actual parameter value provided when SOLVE is called.
X	This array is known throughout SOLVE, SUB1 and SUB2 also. It is local to SOLVE and the programs contained in it, namely SUB1 and SUB2, and is not known outside of SOLVE.
A	This variable appears in all three procedures shown. It is a separate variable in each. In SOLVE it is a parameter to SOLVE, but, because it is declared separately in SUB1 and SUB2, it is a local variable in each of those procedures.
V	This variable is local to SOLVE and not known outside of SOLVE. It is redeclared in SUB1, so the V in SUB1 has no relation to the V in SOLVE. The V in SUB2 is the same as the V in its containing procedure, SOLVE, because it is not redeclared in SUB2.
R and S	These are parameters in SUB1 and SUB2 respectively. They are known only inside those procedures.
SUB1 and SUB2	These procedures are known throughout SOLVE, including the interior of SUB1 and SUB2.

<u>EXTERNAL Identifiers</u>

The rule that an identifier declared within a procedure is local to that procedure can be overridden by the EXTERNAL attribute. If an identifier is declared as EXTERNAL, it is connected by the compiler to any variable of the same name that is also declared as external in another procedure. For example,

```
P: PROCEDURE (...);
    DCL X FIXED DECIMAL EXTERNAL;
    ...
    END P;
Q: PROCEDURE (...);
    DCL X FIXED DECIMAL EXTERNAL;
    ...
    END Q;
```

The variable X in P is the same as the variable X in Q, and will be the same as the variable X in any other procedure in which X is declared EXTERNAL. In large jobs, this facility should be reserved for data that is common to every procedure that is part of the job. Every programmer who makes use of previously written procedures containing external variables must know their names so that they are not used incorrectly. If it is possible to avoid the use of external variables, so much the better. (External identifiers must have names of no more than seven characters and must be STATIC, which is discussed in the next section.)

P10.2 STATIC and AUTOMATIC Storage, and BEGIN Blocks

PL/I variables are AUTOMATIC (dynamic) by default. That is, when a variable is declared inside a procedure, it is allocated space at the time the procedure is called. This is the reason that, in PL/I, we can declare variables with dimensions based on the values of expressions. For example, if a procedure starts with

```
EXMP: PROCEDURE (A, N);
    DCL (N, A, X(N), Y(100)) FIXED DECIMAL;
```

the compiler prepares code which will allocate N cells for the array X at the time the procedure is called. At that time, N has a value. When the procedure terminates, the space allocated to X(N) is free to be allocated to other procedures. The space allocated to the array Y is also free when the procedure is not active, even though we do know how much space is needed. If we want to keep space permanently allocated to variables while the job is in the computer, we must declare the variables to be STATIC. In the example above, this can be done only for Y. A and N are parameters, so they are not associated with storage local to the procedure. The size of X can change from one use of the procedure to another so may not be STATIC, but Y can be declared to be STATIC. This can be done by changing the declaration above to

```
DCL (A, N, X(N)) FIXED DECIMAL,
    Y(100) FIXED DECIMAL STATIC;
```

although we can write it in the form

```
DCL (A, N, X(N), Y(100) STATIC) FIXED DECIMAL;
```

because attributes may be <u>factored</u> in the obvious way. In this example, the attributes FIXED and DECIMAL have been factored out to apply to all four identifiers, while the attribute STATIC has not, so it applies to the variable Y only.

Program P10.1a illustrates the use of STATIC variables and the nesting of procedures described in the previous section for the following task:

> A procedure is to be written which will return a "word" from the input. (A word is defined as any consecutive string of non-blank characters separated by one or more blanks or an end of line.)

The procedure reads the next line using a subprocedure READ_CD. The reason for using a subprocedure is that, if the source of data is changed, only the READ_CD subprocedure must be changed. This effectively isolates the rest of the task from the nature of the data source. Since READ_CD is declared inside READ_WD, a user of READ_WD is unaware of READ_CD. The outer procedure, READ_WD, has a character-string variable which contains the characters read from the last input line. This variable must be static because its value must be retained from one call of READ_WD to another. Since it is not redeclared in READ_CD, it is known to that subprocedure and can be set by it.

Program 10.1a Read the Next Word from the Input Line

```
READ_WD: PROCEDURE (WORD);

    /* SET WORD TO THE NEXT STRING OF NON-BLANK CHARACTERS  */
    /* FROM THE INPUT.  END OF LINE COUNTS AS A BLANK.      */
    /* SET WORD TO '*******' IF THERE IS NO MORE DATA.      */
    DECLARE WORD CHARACTER(*) VARYING,
            BUFFER CHARACTER (256)  VARYING STATIC,
            I FIXED DECIMAL,
            READ_CD ENTRY RETURNS(BIT(1));

    FLOW;
        WORD = '';
        DO WHILE (WORD = '');
            IF BUFFER = ''
                THEN DO;
                    IF READ_CD THEN WORD = '*******'; ELSE;
                    END;
                ELSE DO;
                    /* STRIP LEADING BLANKS FROM BUFFER     */
                    I = VERIFY(BUFFER,' ');
                    IF I ¬= 1
                        THEN BUFFER = SUBSTR(BUFFER,I);
                        ELSE;
                    /* FIND FIRST BLANK IN BUFFER           */
                    I = INDEX(BUFFER, ' ');
                    IF I = 0 THEN I = LENGTH(BUFFER) + 1; ELSE;
                    /* REMOVE NEXT WORD FROM BUFFER         */
                    WORD = SUBSTR(BUFFER,1,I-1);
                    BUFFER = SUBSTR(BUFFER,I);
                    END;
            END;
        RETURN;

    READ_CD: PROCEDURE RETURNS(BIT(1));

        /* READ NEXT LINE, IN THIS CASE A CARD.             */
        /* PLACE INTO BUFFER.  MAXIMUM SIZE IS 256 CHARS.   */
        /* IF END OF FILE IS ENCOUNTERED, RETURNED '1'B,    */
        /* ELSE RETURN '0'B.                                */

        DCL BUF1 CHARACTER(80);
            ON ENDFILE(SYSIN) GO TO LEND;
            GET EDIT (BUF1) (A(80));
            BUFFER = BUF1;
            RETURN ('0'B);
            LEND: RETURN('1'B);
        END READ_CD;
    END READ_WD;
```

BEGIN Blocks

We have seen that variables declared inside procedures are allocated space dynamically as the procedure is entered. There are situations in which we want to allow dynamic allocation of data, particularly arrays, but don't want to use a procedure to achieve it. This is one of the purposes of the BEGIN block. Suppose we want to read in an integer N and then read N items into an array. In many programming languages, we must chose a dimension for the array when we write the program, that is, before we know the actual size, N. Thus we must choose a suitably large value for the size of the array, and hope that no case exceeds that value (although we certainly must program a test to ensure that the program fails gracefully with a message giving the reason). In PL/I, and many other block structured languages, we can read the dimension N and later declare an array with that dimension. For example, if we write

```
...
GET LIST (N);
BEGIN;
    DCL X(N) FLOAT DECIMAL;
    ...
    END;
...
```

the array X is allocated space when the BEGIN block is entered, which occurs immediately after the GET LIST is executed. By that time, N is known so the size of the array can be based on the size of N. The array X, and any variables declared inside the BEGIN block, are only known inside that block. The block extends to its matching END statement. (Since END is used to terminate so many constructions in PL/I, it is a good idea to label some of the larger blocks, and to use the same label after the END, for example,

```
FIND_ZERO: BEGIN;
    declarations
    ...
    END FIND_ZERO;
```

BEGIN blocks can be nested. They affect the scope of identifier definitions in exactly the same way that PROCEDURE definitions do. Variables defined within a BEGIN block are local to that block and AUTOMATIC unless declared otherwise. In many ways, BEGIN blocks can be used where we have been using compound statements of the form DO; ...; END;. However, entering a BEGIN block is more costly in execution time, so should be used only when needed for the declaration of variables.

P10.3 ENTRY points

PL/I subprograms can have additional entry points. They are declared by inserting the ENTRY statement immediately before the first statement to be executed on entry. The ENTRY statement is written in the form

```
name: ENTRY (parameter list);
```

where "name" is the entry point name. Thus, it looks exactly like the initial procedure declaration. Indeed, it may also be followed by the RETURNS (attribute list) qualification if it is used as a function.

Entry points should be used sparingly, and only for special purposes such as initialization. The code used when an entry point is called should be different from the code used when any other entry point (including the principle entry point) is used, or the program will be confusing.

P10.4 Parameters

PL/I parameters are passed by address. If the actual parameter value (argument) is an identifier with the same attributes as the dummy argument in the procedure, the address is the location of the item corresponding to the identifier in memory. Otherwise, it is the address of a temporary. A temporary is a cell (or set of cells) containing the value of the argument in the appropriate form. For example, if the argument is an expression, its value is computed by the calling program and assigned to a temporary. The user should be particularly aware that a temporary is created if the argument has attributes different from the dummy parameter. Suppose, for example, that a procedure has been declared to have a FLOAT DECIMAL argument, and the programmer uses a FIXED DECIMAL variable as the argument. In PL/I, the calling procedure forms the FLOAT DECIMAL form of the argument and places it in a temporary. This means that if the parameter is used for output, the output will be stored in the temporary, and not be stored in the original variable passed as a parameter.

PL/I also passes dimension information and structure information concerning the arguments. This means that if a parameter is an array or a character string, its size does not have to be declared in the subprocedure. The size can be indicated with the asterisk character *. For example, if C is a two dimensional array of character strings that is to be used as a parameter in a procedure, the declaration of C in the procedure can take the form

```
DCL C(*,*) CHARACTER(*);
```

indicating that C has two dimensions, is a character string, and its length will be determined at invocation.

Procedure names and labels can be passed as arguments. Use of labels as arguments is not recommended, but there are good reasons for passing procedure names as arguments. Suppose, for example, that we want to write a procedure which will evaluate a function for a sequence of arguments, and print a table of its values. The procedure could be written as shown in Program P10.2a. The procedure to be passed is given the dummy parameter name SS. It must be declared so that the compiler knows it is a function. When we use this procedure to print a table of the values of a function, we must also declare the function in the calling procedure so that the compiler knows its type and the type of its arguments. For example, if we want to print a table of the values of SIN(X), we must write something like the code shown in Program P10.2b.

Program P10.2a Example of Procedure as Parameter

```
TABLE: PROCEDURE(SS, FIRST, LAST, N);

    /* PRINT A TABLE OF VALUES OF SS                     */
    /* PRINT N VALUES UNIFORMLY BETWEEN FIRST AND LAST   */

    DCL SS ENTRY (FLOAT DECIMAL) RETURNS(FLOAT DECIMAL),
        (FIRST, LAST, X) FLOAT DECIMAL,
        N FIXED DECIMAL;

        IF N = 0
            THEN PUT SKIP LIST ('N TOO SMALL IN TABLE');
            ELSE DO;
                PUT SKIP LIST('X','FUNCTION OF X');
                DO I = 1 TO N;
                    X = FIRST + (LAST - FIRST)*(I-1)/(N-1);
                    PUT SKIP LIST (X, SS(X));
                    END;
                END;
        RETURN;
    END TABLE;
```

P10.2b Use of Program P10.2a to Print a Table of SIN(X)

```
MAIN: PROCEDURE OPTIONS(MAIN);
    DCL TABLE ENTRY (ENTRY (FLOAT DECIMAL) RETURNS (FLOAT DECIMAL),
                    FLOAT DECIMAL, FLOAT DECIMAL, FIXED DECIMAL);
        CALL TABLE (SIN, 0.0E0, 3.14159E0, 5);
        ... definition for TABLE procedure
    END MAIN;
```

Problems

1. Write a procedure with two parameters, A and I, with attributes FLOAT DECIMAL and BIT(1) respectively. Each time it is called with I = '0'B, the value of A should be added to a cumulative total, so that when it is called with I = '1'B, the average of all values of A passed since the last call with I = '1'B can be printed.

2. Change the answer to problem 1 so that it has only the parameter A. Use a separate entry point to cause the procedure to print the average.

3. See what happens when Program P10.3 is coded in PL/I and executed on your system.

Program in text to convert to PL/I: P10.2.

Problems in text to do in PL/I: 6 and 7.

P11 RECURSION IN PL/I

PL/I procedures are non-recursive unless the programmer specifically declares otherwise. This is done by using the keyword RECURSIVE in the PROCEDURE statement. For example,

```
SUB: PROCEDURE(I, J, K) RECURSIVE;
```

indicates that the following lines contain the definition of a recursive procedure called SUB. All other aspects of the definition of recursive procedures are identical to those of non-recursive procedures. This is illustrated in Program P11.1 which is a PL/I version of Program P11.1.

Program P11.1 A Recursive Program to form N + (N-1) + ... + 2 + 1

```
SUB: PROCEDURE(N, M) RECURSIVE;

    DECLARE (N, M, K) FIXED DECIMAL;

        IF N > 1
            THEN DO;
                CALL SUB(N-1, K);
                M = K + N;
                END;
            ELSE M = 1;
        RETURN;
    END SUB;
```

If a recursive function is wanted, the return argument is specified in the usual way after the RETURN keyword. This is illustrated in Program P11.2, which is a PL/I version of Program P11.2.

Program P11.2 Factorial by Recursion

```
FACT: PROCEDURE(N) RECURSIVE RETURNS (FIXED DECIMAL);

    DECLARE N FIXED DECIMAL;

        IF N <= 1 THEN RETURN(1);
            ELSE RETURN (N*FACT(N-1));
    END FACT;
```

Program P11.4 is a PL/I version of Program P11.4. A small change has been made to simplify the program, namely, the simplest case detected is N < 1 rather than N <= 1. If N is less than 1, there is nothing to do, so a return is executed. However, the version in the text will run a little faster because fewer calls of MOVE are executed. The three towers are represented by the integers 1, 2, and 3. The Move Ring statement has been replaced with a print statement that indicates the move made. For example,

```
MOVE RING 3 FROM TOWER 3 TO TOWER 1
```

means that the third smallest ring is moved from the third to the first tower. The output from this program generated by the call statement

```
CALL MOVE(4,1,2)
```

is shown in Table P11.1.

Program P11.4 Towers of Hanoi

```
MOVE: PROCEDURE (N, A, B) RECURSIVE;

    DECLARE (A, B, C, N) FIXED DECIMAL;

        C = 6 - A - B;
        IF N >= 1
            THEN DO;
                CALL MOVE (N-1, A, C);
                PUT SKIP EDIT('MOVE RING',N,' FROM TOWER',A,
                    ' TO TOWER',B)
                    (A,F(4),A,F(2),A,F(2));
                CALL MOVE(N-1,C,B);
                END;
            ELSE;
        RETURN;
    END MOVE;
```

Table P11.1 Output from Program P11.4 for CALL MOVE(4,1,2)

```
MOVE RING   1 FROM TOWER 1 TO TOWER 3
MOVE RING   2 FROM TOWER 1 TO TOWER 2
MOVE RING   1 FROM TOWER 3 TO TOWER 2
MOVE RING   3 FROM TOWER 1 TO TOWER 3
MOVE RING   1 FROM TOWER 2 TO TOWER 1
MOVE RING   2 FROM TOWER 2 TO TOWER 3
MOVE RING   1 FROM TOWER 1 TO TOWER 3
MOVE RING   4 FROM TOWER 1 TO TOWER 2
MOVE RING   1 FROM TOWER 3 TO TOWER 2
MOVE RING   2 FROM TOWER 3 TO TOWER 1
MOVE RING   1 FROM TOWER 2 TO TOWER 1
MOVE RING   3 FROM TOWER 3 TO TOWER 2
MOVE RING   1 FROM TOWER 1 TO TOWER 3
MOVE RING   2 FROM TOWER 1 TO TOWER 2
MOVE RING   1 FROM TOWER 3 TO TOWER 2
```

P11 RECURSION IN PL/I

<u>Problems</u>

1. How many lines does Program <u>P11.4</u> print as a function of N? How many times is MOVE called by MOVE when it is called by another program (as a function of N)?

2. Write a recursive program to scan a text string for matching parentheses. The program should search for a closing parenthesis. If it finds an opening parenthesis, it should call itself to find the matching closing parenthesis for the nested string. The output corresponding to an input text string of

   (ABC(1234)DEFGH(12345(XYZ)678)IJ)

   should be

   1234
   XYZ
   12345678
   ABCDEFGHIJ

   That is, each string in parentheses should be printed as it is found.

<u>Problem in Text to do in PL/I</u>: 1.

<u>Program in Text to Convert to PL/I</u>: P11.3.

A2 THE METHOD OF BISECTION

Program A2.1 computes the zero of the expression giving the amount to be repayed after 24 months on a P percent car loan of $2500 with monthly repayments of $115, as discussed in the text. Recall that this expression is

```
amount left after N months =
  2500*(1 + P/1200)**N - 115*((1 + P/1200)**N - 1)*1200/P
```

The expression is evaluated using the two statements

```
P24 = (1.0 + P/1200.0)**24
F = 2500.0*P24 - 115.0*(P24 - 1.0)*1200.0/P
```

both because it is shorter than a single statement and because evaluating the expression assigned to P24 once rather than twice saves computer time. It uses the method of bisection discussed in A2. The accuracy obtained is at least 0.001.

Program A2.1 Finding the Zero of an Expression

```
ZERO: PROCEDURE OPTIONS(MAIN);
    /* PROGRAM TO COMPUTE EQUIVALENT INTEREST RATE ON        */
    /* 24 MONTH LOAN OF $2500 WITH MONTHLY REPAYMENTS        */
    /* OF $115.                                              */
    DECLARE (LOW, HIGH, P, F, P24) FLOAT DECIMAL;
        LOW = 1.0;
        HIGH = 50.0;
        DO WHILE ((HIGH - LOW) > 0.002E0);
            P = (LOW + HIGH)/2.0;
            P24 = (1 + P/1200.0)**24;
            F = 2500.0*P24 - 115.0*(P24 - 1.0)*1200.0/P;
            IF F > 0.0E0
                THEN HIGH = P;
                ELSE LOW = P;
            END;
        P = (HIGH + LOW)/2.0;
        PUT SKIP LIST ('EFFECTIVE INTEREST RATE IS', P);
    END ZERO;
```

Since the initial distance between LOW and HIGH is 49.0, it is known that 15 passes through the loop will reduce the distance to below 49.0/2**15 which is slightly less than .002, so we could have terminated the loop after fifteen passes instead. This change would not improve the efficiency of the code at all because an additional variable would have to be used as a counter. It would not improve the clarity of the code either, so it is not a worthwhile change.

Problems

1. Change Program A2.1 so that it computes a solution of the equation
   10.0 - 3.0*X - 2.5*X**3 - X**5 = 0.0

2. Change Program A2.1 so that it computes the square root of 2.0 as accurately as possible in the computer being used. (Stop the iteration when there is no further change to LOW and HIGH.)

Problem in text to do in PL/I: 1.

A3 SEARCHING AND SORTING

Program A3.1 is a simple sequential search as given in Program A3.1a. PL/I allows a loop to be continued while two conditions are both true by use of the and combination of two conditions. This is similar to that used in the text, except that the operation and is indicated by the character &. (This is discussed in Section P9.3.)

Program A3.1 Sequential Search

```
SEARCH: PROCEDURE OPTIONS (MAIN);
    DECLARE (ID(100), SCORE (100), IDN, SCN, N, I) FIXED DECIMAL;
        ... code to set values in ID, SCORE and N ...
        GET LIST (IDN, SCN);
        DO WHILE (I <= N & IDN ¬= ID(I));
            I = I + 1;
            END;
        IF I ¬= N + 1 THEN SCORE(I) = SCN; ELSE;
    END SEARCH;
```

A3.1 Binary Search

Program A3.2 is a PL/I version of Program A3.2 which implements the binary search technique in an ordered array.

Program A3.2 Binary Search

```
BINSRCH: PROCEDURE OPTIONS(MAIN);

    /* SEARCH THE ORDERED ARRAY ID(N) FOR THE ELEMENT IDN.  */
    /* SET K TO BE SUCH THAT ID(K) = IDN IF SUCH EXISTS,    */
    /* OTHERWISE, SET K = 0.                                */

    DECLARE (ID(100), IDN, N, LOW, MID, HIGH, K) FIXED DECIMAL;
    ... code to set values in ID etc
        K = 0;
        LOW = 1;
        HIGH = N;
        DO WHILE (LOW <= HIGH & K = 0);
            MID = (LOW + HIGH)/2;
            IF ID(MID) = IDN
                THEN K = MID;
                ELSE IF ID(MID) < IDN
                    THEN LOW = MID + 1;
                    ELSE HIGH = MID - 1;
            PUT SKIP DATA (LOW, HIGH, MID, ID(MID), IDN);
            END;
    END SEARCH;
```

When a program such as this is being debugged, it is helpful to add output statements inside the loop so that the status of important variables can be observed as the program is executed. In the case of Program A3.2, a statement printing LOW, HIGH, MID, and ID(MID) immediately before the END statement in the loop would enable the progress of the program loop to be checked.

A3.2 Sorting

Program A3.5 is a PL/I transliteration of Program A3.5 in the text. It illustrates the use of nested loops.

Program A3.5 Insertion Sort

```
SORT: PROCEDURE OPTIONS(MAIN);

    /* SORT THE ARRAY ID OF N ELEMENTS IN ASCENDING ORDER.  */
    /* N MUST NOT EXCEED 100.                                */

    DECLARE (ID(100), N, J, K, TEMP) FIXED DECIMAL;
     /*   ... code to set information in ID etc */
        K = 1;
        DO WHILE(K <= N-1);
            /* ID(1) TO ID(K) ARE IN ASCENDING ORDER,        */
            /* EXTEND TO ID(K+1).                            */
            IF ID(K) > ID(K+1)
                THEN DO;
                    /* MOVE ID(K+1) BACK TO ITS PROPER       */
                    /* PLACE IN THE ARRAY. FIRST SAVE ITS    */
                    /* VALUE IN TEMP, THEN MOVE EARLIER      */
                    /* ELEMENTS UP ONE PLACE.                */
                    TEMP = ID(K+1);
                    J = K;
                    INNER: DO WHILE(J >= 1 & ID(J) > TEMP);
                        ID(J+1) = ID(J);
                        J = J - 1;
                        END INNER;
                    ID(J+1) = TEMP;
                    END;
                 ELSE;
            K = K + 1;
            END;
            END SORT;
```

Problems

1. Run Program A3.2 with an output statement that prints LOW, HIGH, MID, and ID(MID) before the END of the loop statement. Put 7 elements in the array ID, and search for each in turn. What is the average number of passes through the loop to search for each of the elements? Also search for an element that is not present. How many passes does this take?

2. Insert output statements in Program A3.5 to indicate the state of the array after each pass through the outer loop, and run the program for the data 3,5,2,7,4,6,1.

Programs in text to convert to PL/I: A3.3 with A3.3a, and A3.4

A4 POINTERS AND CHAINED LISTS

The only way that chained lists can be implemented in PL/C is by the use of arrays as described in the text. PL/I has a data type called POINTER which can be used instead. It is described very briefly in Section P9.4, but will not be used here because it involves too many additional language features for a beginning student. Programs A4.1 and A4.2 are given below in PL/I form with some explanatory remarks.

Program A4.1 Initialize a free list

```
... surrounding procedure ...
DECLARE (PTR(N), AVAIL) FIXED DECIMAL;
...

INIT: PROCEDURE;

    /* INITIAL FREE STORAGE IN THE ARRAY PTR                 */
    /* SET THE FREE START IN AVAIL                           */
    /* AND THE LIST HEAD IN PTR(1) TO 0                      */

    DECLARE I FIXED DECIMAL;
        AVAIL = 2;
        PTR(1) = 0;
        DO I = 2 TO N - 1;
            PTR(I) = I + 1;
            END;
        PTR(N) = 0;
        RETURN;
    END INIT;
```

Program A4.1 indicates that the subroutine INIT has no parameters, but is contained in a procedure which declares PTR, AVAIL, and N. Hence these are known to INIT and do not have to be passed and declared internally. Since the set of procedures will probably be used to manipulate a single data structure, this saves writing and the time to pass parameters. However, if several sets of lists were to be manipulated in a single job, it would be better to pass the identifiers as parameters, as done in the text.

Similarly, in Program A4.2, the identifiers PTR, DATA, AVAIL, and N are assumed to be declared in a surrounding procedure. The name to be added, NAME, is passed as a parameter, however, as it is quite likely that the list addition program could be called from several places to add different names. This program does not use the statement

```
DO WHILE (PTR(I) ¬= 0 & DATA(PTR(I)) < NAME);
```

because, although this is a syntactically valid statement in PL/I, it can cause errors if PTR(I) is zero and subscript ranges are being checked. Instead, the test is done in two stages, using a loop exit fashioned from an IF and a GO TO.

Programs in text to convert to PL/I: A4.3 and A4.4.

Problems in text to do in PL/I: 1, 2, 3, 5, 6, and 7.

Program A4.2 Add an Element to an Ordered List

```
ADD: PROCEDURE (NAME);

    /* INSERT NAME IN ORDER LIST THROUGH PTR AND DATA.          */
    /* THE LIST HEAD IS IN PTR(1)                               */

    DECLARE I FIXED DECIMAL, NAME CHARACTER(*);
        IF AVAIL = 0
            THEN PUT SKIP LIST ('NO LIST SPACE IN ADD');
            ELSE DO;
                I = 1;
                DO WHILE (PTR(I) ¬= 0);
                    J = PTR(I);
                    IF DATA(J) >= NAME THEN GO TO LOOP_EXIT; ELSE;
                        /* EXIT LOOP */
                    I = J;
                    END;
                LOOP_EXIT:
                J = AVAIL;
                AVAIL = PTR(J);
                PTR(J) = PTR(I);
                DATA(J) = NAME;
                PTR(I) = J;
                END;
        RETURN;
    END ADD;
```

A11 SIMULATION

Many problem oriented languages are available for simulation. A number of these are intimately connected to procedural languages such as Fortran or PL/I. In this case, the procedural language is called the host language. The processor for the problem oriented language converts problem statements into host language subroutines for subsequent execution. This makes it possible for a user to write part of the problem--the part that describes the procedure to be followed in the simulation process--in the host language. Because PL/I is well suited for scientific programming, it is not difficult to program a number of simple simulation tasks directly in PL/I, thus avoiding the use of large simulation packages. This is particularly true for continuous simulation of simple problems such as the chemistry problem described in the text. In fact, most computer installations provide a number of subroutines which solve the differential equations of many such problems. We will not discuss those here, but illustrate the use of PL/I for continuous and discrete system simulation.

A11.1 Continuous Simulation

Program A11.1 is a PL/I version of the corresponding program in the text, adapted for batch use. A number of simplifications have been made. In particular, the computation of one of the variables, q, is done indirectly using a relation called a "conservation" relation. In this problem we observe that the amount p + q + r is constant because each time that one gram of material P combines with one gram of material Q, 2 grams of material R are produced. (That is, the total weight of all materials present doesn't change, or is conserved.) The expression p + q + r is called an invariant because it doesn't change. If we compute the initial value of p + q + r, we can always find the value of q when we know the values of p and r.

The program contains an infinite loop so that it can process any number of cases. The output of each case begins on a new page with the printing of the input data appropriately labelled. This is very important as it enables the user to check that the correct data was input for each case. An edit-directed I/O statement is used to describe the initial values. It is convenient to associate each new line of output with one or more lines in the I/O list and the format description. Although this is not required, it enables the format to be changed easily.

A11.2 Discrete Simulation

Program P11.4 is a PL/I version of Program P11.4 which simulates the behavior of the arrival line at a bank. The changes suggested in Chapter A11 for simulating a single arrival line have been made. Note that the changes are made in such a way that they can be removed easily. The additional program lines for the two arrival line simulation are in the program, but have been converted to comments by punching the comment quotes around them. The PL/C function RAND is used for random number generation. This is not a part of PL/I, so if PL/C is not being used, RAND must be replaced with a locally available random number generator. RAND is a function of one argument, say X. X normally contains the value of the previous random number generated. A new one can be obtained by writing "X = RAND(X);".

Program in text to convert to PL/I: A11.2.

Problems in text to do in PL/I: 1 and 2.

Program A11.1 Continuous Simulation Example

```
CHEMIST: PROCEDURE OPTIONS(MAIN);

    /*  PROGRAM TO SIMULATE A CHEMICAL REACTION              */
    /*  INITIAL DATA SHOULD BE SPECIFIED AS FOLLOWS:         */
    /*    FIRST CARD:                                        */
    /*     VALUES OF REACTION RATES ALPHA AND BETA           */
    /*    SECOND CARD:                                       */
    /*     INITIAL VALUES OF P, Q, AND R                     */
    /*    THIRD CARD:                                        */
    /*     LENGTH OF SIMULATED RUN (SECS) AND NUMBER OF      */
    /*     STEPS/SEC.                                        */

    DCL (ALPHA, BETA, P, Q, R, SUM, DP) FLOAT DECIMAL,
            (I, TN, J, M) FIXED DECIMAL;
    /* PROGRAM TERMINATES ON END OF INPUT DATA               */

    NEW_CASE: DO WHILE('1'B);
        GET LIST (ALPHA, BETA);
        GET LIST (P, Q, R);
        GET LIST (TN, M);
        I = 0;
        PUT EDIT ('REACTION RATES ARE',
            'ALPHA =',ALPHA,'  BETA =',BETA,
            'SIMULATION IS DONE',M,' TIMES PER/SEC',
            'TIME SECS','P','Q','R',
            I, P, Q, R)
            (PAGE,A,SKIP,A,E(15,5),A,E(15,5),SKIP,
             A,F(5),A,SKIP(2),A(15),A(15),A(15),A(1),SKIP(2),
             F(10),(3)E(15,5));
        SUM = P + Q + R;
        DO I = 1 TO TN;
            ONE_SEC_LOOP: DO J = 1 TO M;
                DP = (BETA*R - ALPHA*P*Q)/M;
                P = P + DP;
                R = R - 2.0*DP;
                Q = SUM - P - R;
                END ONE_SEC_LOOP;
            PUT SKIP EDIT(I, P, Q, R) (F(10),(3) E(15,5));
            END;
        END NEW_CASE;
    END CHEMIST;
```

Program P11.4 Bank Drive-up Line Simulation

```
BANKSIM: PROCEDURE OPTIONS(MAIN);

/* A TWO-TELLER DRIVE-UP BANK FACILITY IS SIMULATED     */
/* A SINGLE LINE IS USED FOR WAITING CARS               */
/* STRING QUOTES FROM LINES FOLLOWING LINES CONTAINING  */
/* '*********************************************'     */
/* VARIABLE USAGE INCLUDES                              */
/*   BUSY(I)     TELLER I IS BUSY IF TRUE               */
/*   TELTIME(I), I=1,2  TIME WHEN TELLER I NEXT FREE    */
/*   ARRTIME     TIME AT WHICH NEXT ARRIVAL OCCURS      */
/*   QLENGTH(I) # OF CUSTOMERS IN                       */
/*               LINE I, INCLUDING CUSTOMER AT WINDOW   */
/*               (NOT USED IN SINGLE LINE SIMULATION)   */
/*   LIST STRUCTURE: (PTR, CUST_ARR_TIME, SERVICE_TIME) */
/*               CONTAINING POINTERS, ARRIVAL TIMES,    */
/*               AND SERVICE TIMES OF CUSTOMERS.        */
/*   PTR(I), I = 1,2  LIST HEADS FOR LINES 1 AND 2      */
/*   LIST_END(I), I = 1,2 END OF LISTS 1 AND 2          */
/*   FREE_START          START OF FREE_START LIST       */

DCL (TELTIME(2),TIME,ARRTIME,WAIT,WAITSQ,
        STPTIM, LENGTH) FLOAT DECIMAL;
DCL (QLENGTH(2), LIST_END(2), FREE_START, NCUSTS, I)
                                      FIXED DECIMAL;
DCL BUSY(2) BIT(1):
DCL 1 LIST(100),
    2 PTR FIXED DECIMAL,
    2 (CUST_ARR_TIME,SERVICE_TIME) FLOAT DECIMAL;

    CALL INITIALIZE;
    /* INPUT THE LENGTH OF THE SIMULATION RUN           */
    TIME = 0.0E0;
    GET LIST (LENGTH);
    DO WHILE (LENGTH > 0);
        STOP_TIME = TIME + LENGTH;
        WAIT = 0.0E0;
        WAITSQ = 0.0E0;
        NCUSTS = 0;
        DO WHILE (TIME < STOP_TIME);
            /* SET I TO INDEX OF NEXT EVENT.            */
            /* VALUES ARE: I = 0 -- NEW ARRIVAL         */
            /* I = 1 OR 2 -- DEPARTURE FROM TELLER I    */
            T = ARRTIME;
            I = 0;
            IF T > TELTIME(1) & BUSY(1)
                THEN DO;
                    T = TELTIME(1);
                    I = 1;
                    END;
                ELSE;
            IF T > TELTIME(2) & BUSY(2) THEN I = 2; ELSE;
            IF I = 0
                THEN DO;
                    TIME = ARRTIME;
                    CALL ARRIVAL;
                  END;
```

```
                ELSE DO;
                    TIME = TELTIME(I);
                    CALL TELLER(I);
                   END;
            END;
        PUT EDIT ('SIMULATION FOR LENGTH', LENGTH,
                '# CUSTOMERS ARRIVED', NCUSTS,
                'AVERAGE WAIT TIME', WAIT/NCUSTS,
                'AVERAGE SQUARE WAIT TIME', WAITSQ/NCUSTS)
                (SKIP(2),(2)(A(26),F(10),SKIP),
                 (2)(A(26),F(10,4),SKIP));
        GET SKIP LIST (LENGTH);
        END;

TELLER: PROCEDURE (I);

/* THIS PROGRAM IS CALLED IF TELLER I HAS JUST FINISHED */
/* SERVING A CUSTOMER, OR IF TELLER I IS FREE_START AND A        */
/* CUSTOMER HAS BEEN ADDED TO THE SYSTEM.                */
/* IT MOVES A CUSTOMER TO THE TELLER WINDOW IF ONE       */
/* IS WAITING.                                           */

    DCL (I, J, K) FIXED DECIMAL;
        K = 1;
/* **************************************************** */
/*      K = I;                                           */
        IF BUSY(I) THEN QLENGTH(K) = QLENGTH(K) - 1;
        IF PTR(K) ¬= 0
            THEN DO;
                /* LINE NOT EMPTY, MOVE CUSTOMER TO      */
                /* TELLER WINDOW.                        */
                J = PTR(K);
                TELTIME(I) = TIME + SERVICE_TIME(J);
                WAIT = WAIT + TIME - CUST_ARR_TIME(J);
                WAITSQ = WAITSQ + (TIME - CUST_ARR_TIME(J))**2;
                NCUSTS = NCUSTS + 1;
                /* REMOVE ENTRY AND ADD TO FREE STORAGE */
                PTR(K) = PTR(J);
                IF PTR(K) = 0 THEN LIST_END(K) = K; ELSE;
                BUSY(I) = '1'B;
                PTR(J) = FREE_START;
                FREE_START = J;
                END;
            ELSE BUSY(I) = '0'B;
        RETURN;
    END TELLER;
```

```
    ARRIVAL: PROCEDURE;

    /* HANDLE A NEW ARRIVAL.  COMPUTE SERVICE TIME          */
    /* AND TIME OF NEXT ARRIVAL.  ADD TO APPROPRIATE LINE.  */

    DCL X FLOAT DECIMAL STATIC INITIAL (0.1234567);
    DCL (I, J, K) FIXED DECIMAL;

        IF FREE_START = 0
            THEN DO;
                PUT SKIP LIST
                    ('NO FREE_START SPACE, SIMULATION ABORTED');
                TIME = 1.0E50;
                END;
            ELSE DO;
                I = FREE_START;
                FREE_START = PTR(I);
                X = RAND(X);
                SERVICE_TIME(I) = 1.0 + 9.0*X;
                X = RAND(X);
                ARRTIME = TIME + 2.0 + 4.0*X;
                J = 1;
            /* ********************************************** */
            /*  IF QLENGTH(2) < QLENGTH(1) THEN J = 2;ELSE; */
                /* ADD NEW CUSTOMER TO LINE J                  */
                PTR(I) = 0;
                CUST_ARR_TIME(I) = TIME;
                QLENGTH(J) = QLENGTH(J) + 1;
                PTR(LIST_END(J)) = I;
                LIST_END(J) = I;
                IF -BUSY(1)
                    THEN CALL TELLER(1);
                    ELSE IF ¬BUSY(2) THEN CALL TELLER(2); ELSE;
                RETURN;
        END ARRIVAL;

    INITIALIZE: PROCEDURE;

    /* INITIALIZE DATA STRUCTURE AND GLOBAL VARIABLES.      */

    DCL I FIXED DECIMAL;
        DO I = 1 TO 2;
            LIST_END(I) = I;
            PTR(I) = 0;
            QLENGTH(I) = 0;
            BUSY(I) = '0'B;
            TELTIME(I) = 0.0E0;
            END;
        DO I = 3 TO 99;
            PTR(I) = I + 1;
            END;
        PTR(100) = 0;
        FREE_START = 3;
        ARRTIME = 0.0E0;
        RETURN;
    END INITIALIZE;
END BANKSIM;
```

PART C A REFERENCE TO PL/I AND PL/C

This part contains a list of all PL/I statements covered in previous parts plus a summary of the rules governing their use. It is intended as a reference to help answer questions that may arise. To keep this part to a reasonable size, and to avoid confusing the beginning programmer, not all of either PL/C or PL/I is covered. If the reader needs answers to further questions about PL/I, the supplier's language manual should be consulted. (This is usually a very long, complex document.) For the IBM PL/I compilers, the appropriate manual is OS PL/I Checkout and Optimizing Compilers Language Reference Manual, while for PL/C, you should consult User's Guide to PL/C, The Cornell Compiler for PL/I. Both of these are listed in the bibliography at the end of Part C.

This part is organized into four chapters. Chapter C1 provides definitions of many of the terms used (for example, identifier), and can be used much as a glossary. Chapter C1 also gives a concise discussion of many aspects of PL/I that are common to many statements, such as conversion. Chapter C2 lists all PL/I statements covered in the text in alphabetical order, and gives a short description of their usage. All material covered in Chapters C1 and C2 are common to both PL/I and PL/C unless specifically noted otherwise. Chapter C3 is a reference list of most of the built-in functions available to the PL/I and PL/C users, while C4 describes some of the differences between PL/I and PL/C.

General Comments

In the description of PL/I that follows, we will frequently state that a particular data type is required. For example, an array element is of the form Z(integer, ..., integer), where each of the indices is an integer. PL/I is very "forgiving" in the sense that it will accept almost any type of data and convert the data provided to the correct form. For example, if we wrote Z(1.5,2.7), the two non-integer indices are converted to integers by truncation automatically. If nothing is said otherwise, you can assume that an automatic conversion of type is done for you by PL/I. However, you should check the conversion rules given in Chapter C1 to be certain that you understand those situations in which you can lose accuracy or run into other difficulties.

In the descriptions that follow, items in capital letters are PL/I or PL/C keywords, or examples of PL/I programs.

C1 DEFINITIONS OF SOME PL/I TERMS

Alphabetic Characters - The letters A to Z and the three characters $, #, and @.

Alphanumeric Characters - The alphabetic characters and the decimal digits 0 through 9.

Arithmetic Operators - The operators +, -, *, / and ** (for addition, subtraction, multiplication, division, and exponentiation respectively). + and - may be used as unary operators. See Expressions for rules concerning use of these operators.

Array - An array is a collection of variables under the same name. The elements of an array are identified by an index. A one-dimensional array has one index, so its Ith element can be referred to as NAME(I), if the name of the array is NAME. The size of an array is declared when the variable is declared by following the name with a list of index ranges. For example, DECLARE A(i11:i12, i21:i22, ..., im1,im2) ... declares A to have m dimensions. The range of the jth dimension is ij1 to ij2. If the lowest index value is one, it can be omitted, along with the following colon.

Array Element - An array name followed by a parenthesized list of integer index expressions, each expression separated by a comma. The number of index expressions must equal the number of dimensions.

Attributes - Every PL/I variable or constant has a set of one or more attributes. The attributes describe the way the item is used. The attributes of constants are determined from the way they are written. (For example, 3.45E6 is DECIMAL FLOAT because it is written in decimal with an exponent.) The attributes of variables should be declared, although PL/I does allow some to be assumed by default. In the description below, we specifically indicate those attributes that can be assumed by default, namely REAL, AUTOMATIC, INTERNAL, and, for program label constants, LABEL. In the interests of good programming style, all other attributes should be declared specifically. Because PL/I does accept default declarations, it is possible that the programmer can forget a declaration and be unaware of the fact. Therefore, one should check the usage list printed by the compiler to make sure that no variables have been declared totally by default.

The _type_ attributes specify the type of data that can be stored in a variable, or form a constant. Other attributes indicate when and where the variable can be used. The type attributes of arithmetic data are:

base - DECIMAL or BINARY. One of these should be specified.
scale - FIXED or FLOAT. One of these should be specified.
mode - REAL or COMPLEX. REAL is the default, and need not be specified.
precision - not in general needed. Allows the number of digits in a numerical value to be specified. See Precision.

The type attribute of string data is either BIT or CHARACTER, possibly modified by VARYING--meaning varying length. Labels have an type attribute of LABEL.

Other attributes are:

storage class - Either AUTOMATIC or STATIC indicating whether the variable is only allocated space when the block in which it is defined is active or for all time. AUTOMATIC is the default condition, and it not usually specified.

scope - Either INTERNAL or EXTERNAL, indicating whether the variable is known outside of the program block in which it is defined or not. INTERNAL is the default, and is not usually specified.

INITIAL - specifies the initial value of the variable, if any.

LABEL - indicates that the value is a program label. Identifiers appearing on program statements are LABEL constants. A LABEL variable must be specifically declared, in which case it can be assigned LABEL values. (However, such programming is not generally recommended.)

Bit String Operators - The three operators ¬, &, and |, standing for *not*, *and*, and *or* respectively, operate on bit strings. A bit string is a string of zero or more bits. The operator *not* complements each bit in the string, that is, ¬'101100'B is '010011'B. The operators *and* and *or* perform the logical operations on bits in the corresponding positions in the two strings. That is, if X and Y are each 5-bit string, X&Y is a 5-bit string whose jth bit is the *and* of the jth bits of X and Y. If one operand is shorter than the other, it is extended *on the right* with zero bits to make it the same length as the other before the operation.

The relational operators and the concatenation operator may also be used on bit strings. In a relational operation, the shorter string is extended with zeros *on the right* to make it the same length as the longer, and then the two strings are compared as positive integers. The result is '1'B if the relation is true, '0'B otherwise. Concatenation forms a bit string whose length is the sum of the lengths of the two operands, and whose value is the first string followed by the second. For example, '101'B||'0100'B is '1010100'B.

Blanks - Blank characters have no effect on PL/I statements provided that they do not appear within an identifier, keyword, or constant. They must be used to separate identifiers and keywords from each other. They can, and should, be used to improve readability by indentation.

Block - A block of code surrounded by BEGIN and END. Is used to allow variables to be declared locally to the block.

Character Strings - PL/I character strings are declared either as fixed length using the attribute CHARACTER(length), where the length is between 1 and 256, or as varying in length with a maximum size specified using the attributes CHARACTER(max-length) VARYING. The maximum length is also restricted to between 1 and 256.

Character String Operators - The binary operations of concatenation and comparison can be performed on character strings. Concatenation is represented by ||, and the comparison operators are the usual relational operators. If X and Y are character strings, X||Y is a character string whose length is the sum of the lengths of X and Y. The relational operators are performed by first extending the shorter string with blanks on the right until it has the length of the longer string, and then comparing them in the usual lexical sense. The collating sequence used is

```
ƀ.<(+|&$*);¬-/,%_>?:#=AB...Z01...9
```

where ƀ is the blank character.

Comments - Comments can appear anywhere that a blank can appear. They must be surrounded by the "brackets" /* and */. In PL/C, a comment should not cross a card boundary (although that restriction can be optionally removed).

Compound Statement - Many PL/I structures, for example, IF - THEN - ELSE, allow a single unit such as a statement or compound statement to appear after the THEN and ELSE keywords. A compound statement is a list of statements or other program units (e.g. compound statements) preceded by the keyword DO and followed by END. Whenever the single unit should be executed, each of the units in the compound statement is executed in order.

Condition prefix A statement, block, or procedure may be preceded by one or more condition prefixes. They are enclosed in parentheses and followed by a colon. Prefixes include the following. Each of these may be prefixed with the letters NO to inhibit the condition in the block or procedure to which they apply, even though the condition is enabled for an outer block.

CHECK(list) where list is a list of variable and/or label identifiers. Each time one of the variables listed is changed, or one of the labels listed is on a statement that is executed, printing occurs, indicating the new value of the variable or the statement number executed.

FIXEDOVERFLOW Enables checking for fixed point overflow.

FLOW (PL/C only) Enables a flow trace of the program inside the block or procedure to which it applies.

OVERFLOW Enables overflow checking.

SUBSCRIPTRANGE Enables checking of subscript ranges. Normally on in PL/C but off in PL/I.

UNDERFLOW Enables checking for underflow.

ZERODIVIDE Enables checking for attempted division by zero.

Constants Constants can have any of the attributes of simple variables, such as FLOAT, FIXED, DECIMAL, BINARY, COMPLEX, CHARACTER string, BIT string, or LABEL. They are represented as follows:

BINARY - If a numerical constant is followed by the letter B, it is interpreted as a binary constant, in which case, all the digits of a FIXED constant, or all the digits of the mantissa of a FLOAT constant must be 0 or 1. The point, if present, is a binary point, while the exponent, if present, indicates the power of two by which the mantissa should be multiplied. However, note that the exponent itself is represented in decimal. Thus, 1.01011E+3B is the same as 1010.11E0B, which has the value 10.75E0.

BIT string - a string of 0 and 1 characters, surrounded by quotes and followed by the letter B. For example, '10101100'B is an eight-bit string.

CHARACTER String - (also called a literal) is any string of characters surrounded by single quotes. For example, 'ABC123' is a six-character string. (If a quote is to appear in the string, it must be represented by two quotes; thus, 'IT''S' represents the four-character string IT'S.)

COMPLEX - in PL/I, a complex constant is specified as the sum of a real part and an imaginary part. An imaginary part is formed by appending the letter I to the end of any real numerical constant. Thus, 45.3E0 + 2.45E3I is the complex number whose real and imaginary parts are 0.453E2 and 0.245E4 respectively.

DECIMAL - A FIXED or FLOAT constant is taken to be DECIMAL unless followed by a B to indicate BINARY.

FIXED - signed or unsigned digit string with or without point, but without exponent. The precision is determined by the number of digits used.

FLOAT - signed or unsigned digit string with or without point specifies the mantissa. It must be followed by an exponent written as Esn, where s is an optional sign and n is the exponent represented as a decimal integer.

C1 DEFINITIONS OF SOME PL/I TERMS

LABEL - a label constant is any indentifier that has been defined as a label by having been used as such. It appears in front of a statement and is separated from the statement by a colon. It can be passed as a parameter, or assigned to a label variable.

Logical - in PL/I, logical values are represented as one-bit bit strings. Therefore, true is the same as '1'B, while false is the same as '0'B.

Conversion - When data of one type is provided for an operation that expects data of another type, PL/I normally converts the data appropriately. This is convenient when arithmetic data is involved, but not always desirable when other data, such as a character string, is mixed with arithmetic data. Such mixing frequently indicates a program error, and it would be better if it were detected by the compiler. Therefore, we will describe only those automatic conversions that should be used. (If the data is provided as a parameter to a subprocedure, the type of arguments expected in the subprocedure must have been declared in a block or procedure containing the call or function reference, otherwise the automatic conversion will not occur in PL/I, but may occur in PL/C. Built-in functions need not be so declared, because PL/I is aware of the data types of their arguments.) Generally, data conversion occurs because a binary arithmetic operation has operands of different types. In this case, they are converted to the "higher" type as follows:

Decimal becomes binary if either is binary.
Fixed becomes float if either is float.
(Float**integer is evaluated directly without conversion.)
Fixed**fixed is evaluated in floating point unless the exponent is an integer.
Real becomes complex if either is complex.
(Complex**integer is evaluated directly by multiplication.)

Conversion also occurs when the type of the expression on the right of an assignment statement differs from the type of variable on the left-hand side. The following cases are important:

Real = Complex	The imaginary part is discarded
Complex = Real	A zero imaginary part is added
Fixed = Float	May cause loss of accuracy by truncation
Float = Fixed	May cause loss of accuracy by truncation
Decimal = Binary	Causes no problem in floating point but can cause loss of leading digits in fixed point (because of difference in range of representations)

Conversion between bit and character strings occurs when they appear together, or if a character string appears in a bit-string operation. The rules are:

A bit string is converted to a character string of zeros and ones of the same length. A character string should contain only zero and one characters, and is converted to a bit string of the same length. If the character string contains other characters, an error condition (called CONVERSION) is caused.

Data Types - all data, whether variable or constant, has a set of <u>attributes</u>, which we have been referring to loosely as the data type.

Expression - A string of constants, variables, array elements, and/or expressions enclosed in parentheses separated by operators. The precedence of the operators is listed under operators. An automatic conversion of data type occurs if (a) the operator expects a certain type of data and something else is supplied, or (b) a binary operator will take several different types of data, and two different types are provided. See Conversion.

File name - An identifier used to refer to a file of data on an I/O device. Standard file names are SYSIN and SYSPRINT for the standard input and output files. Any other files must be declared to the operating system in a way which is system dependent and not part of the language. Other file names must also be declared in a DECLARATION statement with the attribute FILE.

Identifiers - A PL/I identifier is a string of one or more characters. The first character must be alphabetic. The remaining characters can be alphanumeric or break characters. The maximum length of a identifier depends on its usage. For example, internal variable names may not exceed 31 characters, external names may not exceed 7 characters.

Keywords - PL/I has a large number of keywords. Some of these are reserved words in PL/C, but not in PL/I. Some keywords may be abbreviated. The list below gives those keywords that are reserved in PL/I and those that can be abbreviated. If an abbreviation may be used for the keyword, it appears in brackets following the keyword. An asterisk precedes those that are reserved in PL/C.

*ALLOCATE *BEGIN BINARY [BIN] *BY *CALL CHARACTER [CHAR] *CHECK *CLOSE DECIMAL [DEC] *DECLARE [DCL] *DELETE *DO *ELSE *END *ENTRY *EXIT FIXEDOVERFLOW [FOFL] *FLOW *FORMAT *FREE *GET *GO *GOTO *IF INITIAL [INIT] *NO *NOCHECK *NOFLOW *ON *OPEN OVERFLOW [OFL] POINTER [PTR] *PROCEDURE [PROC] *PUT *READ *RETURN *REVERT *REWRITE *SIGNAL *STOP SUBSCRIPTRANGE [SUBRG] *THEN *TO UNDERFLOW [UFL] *WHILE *WRITE ZERODIVIDE [ZDIV]

Label - The name of a position in the program. Takes the form of an identifier of up to 31 characters. LABEL is also a possible attribute of a variable.

Literals - Literals are character string constants. See CONSTANTS.

Logical Operators - See Bit String Operators.

Logical Values - The logical values true and false are represented as the one-bit strings '1'B and '0'B respectively.

Numeric Characters - The decimal digits 0 through 9.

Operators - The set of Arithmetic, Bit-String, Relational, and Character-String operators. The precedence of these operators is

```
** ¬ unary + or -            highest
 *    /
 +    -
    ||
<  >  =  ¬=  >=  <=  ¬<  ¬>
    &
    |                         lowest
```

Operators at the same level are performed left-to-right _except_ for the top level,which are performed right-to-left.

Precision - The number of digits (decimal or binary) in a value. Throughout this manual we have used the default precisions. However, the programmer can declare the precision and override these defaults. In fixed point, the declaration takes the form

```
DCL VAR xxx FIXED(p,d);
```

where xxx is BINARY or DECIMAL, p is the total number of digits, and d is the number of digits after the point. If d is zero, the comma and d can be omitted. The maximum precision is 15 in DECIMAL and 31 in BINARY. In floating point, the declaration takes the form

```
DCL VAR xxx FLOAT(p);
```

where p is the number of digits in the mantissa, with a maximum of 16 for DECIMAL and 53 for BINARY. The default precisions used in IBM PL/I are:

```
FIXED DECIMAL  (5,0)
FLOAT DECIMAL  (6)
FIXED BINARY   (15,0)
FLOAT BINARY   (21)
```

Qualified Name - See Structures.

Record — A single block of data that is read or written from or on an I/O device in one operation. The information on a single card or single printer line is one record.

Relational Operators - The operators are

```
>              for greater than
>=  or ¬<      for greater than or equal
<              for less than
<=  or ¬>      for less than or equal
=              for equal
-=             for not equal
```

They all have the same precedence. See Operators for their precedence relative to other operators. The result is a logical value, that is, a bit string of length one.

Statement - PL/I recognizes a number of statements. A statement either tells the compiler a fact about the program (non-executable statement) or is an instruction to perform some action at execution time (executable statement). A statement is punched in columns 2 through 72 of any number of cards or lines. It is terminated by a semicolon.

Structure - A set of variables arranged so that either one or specified subsets can be referenced as a unit. A structure consists of a set of one or more substructures, where each substructure is a variable or structure, as in

```
DECLARE EMPLOYEE (100),
          2 NAME CHAR(20),
          2 WAGE_RATE FIXED DECIMAL (5,2),
          2 PERSONAL_DATA
             3 AGE FIXED DECIMAL (2),
             3 ADDRESS CHAR(40),
             3 BANK_NAME CHAR(30),
          2 TAX_DATA,
             3 MONTHS_WAGES (12) FIXED DECIMAL (9,2),
             3 TAX_TO_DATE FIXED DECIMAL (8,2);
```

Here, EMPLOYEE is an array of 100 structures, each consisting of four substructures, namely, the two simple variables NAME and WAGE_RATE and the two substructures PERSONAL_DATA and TAX_DATA. The latter are, in turn, sets of substructures, consisting of three simple variables and a simple variable and an array of 12 entries respectively. A reference to a structure or substructure references every element in that structure or substructure. Thus, PERSONAL_DATA refers to the set of 100 items called PERSONAL_DATA for all 100 employees. If the identifier PERSONAL_DATA is used as the name of other data, for example in another structure, the name must be qualified. EMPLOYEE.PERSONAL_DATA refers to the set of PERSONAL_DATA that is a part of the structure EMPLOYEE. EMPLOYEE(5).PERSONAL_DATA refers to the PERSONAL_DATA of the fifth EMPLOYEE. EMPLOYEE(11).TAX_DATA.MONTHS_WAGES(4) refers to the fourth entry in the array MONTHS_WAGES for the eleventh EMPLOYEE.

Variable - A cell or set of cells in memory which contain values that can change during the execution of the program. Variables have names by which they can be referenced. The name is an identifier of no more than 31 characters (7 if it is an external variable). A simple variable has a single value, while an array or structure is equivalent to a set of simple variables.

C2 PL/I STATEMENTS

This chapter summarizes the basic PL/I statements. They are listed alphabetically for reference. Illustrations are given in part P of this manual.

Array Assignment - If an assignment statement references an array, the assignment statement will be executed for each member of the array. For example, if X, Y, and Z are each 10 by 20 element arrays, X = Y + Z; will assign Y(I,J) + Z(I,J) to X(I,J) for I = 1 TO 10 and J = 1 TO 20. It is equivalent to the statements

```
DO I = 1 TO 10;
  DO J = 1 TO 20;
     X(I,J) = Y(I,J) + Z(I,J);
     END;
  END;
```

Note that the assignment statements are executed in row order. All operands in the array assignment statement must have exactly the same dimension, or be simple variables. For example, if X is dimensioned as before, X = X - X(3,3); subtracts the old value of X(3,3) from the first two rows and the first three elements of the third row of X. Thereafter, it does not change the remaining elements of X because X(3,3) is set to zero before the assignment is executed for the latter elements.

Assignment - An assignment statement takes the form

```
left-hand-side = right-hand-side;
```

The right-hand side can be any expression, while the left-hand side must be the name of a cell or cells that receives the result. If the type of the right-hand side differs from that of the left-hand side, a conversion occurs. (See Conversion in C1 and Array and Structure Assignment in this chapter.)

BEGIN ... END - These statements surround a block of code within which variables can be declared that are local to the block. The usual form is

```
BEGIN;
  declarations
    list of executable statements
  END;
```

The identifiers declared within the block are not known outside of the block (unless they are declared to be EXTERNAL). Blocks may be nested within other blocks. A label may be placed on the BEGIN. In that case, the same label may follow the END. For example,

```
SWITCH: BEGIN;
    ...
    END SWITCH;
```

CALL - The CALL statement invokes a subroutine. It takes the form

```
CALL name(argument list);
```

where name is the name of the subroutine and argument list is a list of actual parameter values separated with commas. Chapter P10 describes the way parameters are passed in PL/I.

CHECK A PL/C statement. Turns the CHECK condition on. Can be followed by an expression in parentheses. The expression is evaluated and the CHECK condition is enabled for that number of times.

DECLARE - The declaration statement is used to specify the nature of all variables used by the program. It can also be used to specify initial values of those variables. The general form is

```
DECLARE declaration-1,
        declaration-2,
        ...
        declaration-n;
```

where each declaration-i has the form

```
variable-list   specification
```

Variable-list is either a single identifier or a list of identifiers, separated by commas and surrounded by parentheses, while specifiation is a list of one or more attributes. Arrays are declared by following the identifier with the dimension of the array, written in the form (lower-1:upper-1, ..., lower-k,upper-k), where lower-i and upper-i are the lower and upper bounds of the i-th dimension. These bounds may be expressions, but the upper bound must not be less than the lower bound. If the lower bound is one, it and the following colon can be omitted. Arithmetic data should be assigned one of each of the pairs of attributes

FIXED or FLOAT
DECIMAL or BINARY
REAL or COMPLEX
AUTOMATIC or STATIC
INTERNAL or EXTERNAL

although the first cases of the last three need not be specified as they are default cases. A STATIC variable is one that is permanently assigned storage, even when the containing block or procedure is not active. AUTOMATIC variables, the default case, lose their values when a procedure or block is exitted. EXTERNAL variables can be referenced by any other block or procedure that declares the same name as EXTERNAL. Such variables must be STATIC, and their names may not exceed seven characters. The precision of arithmetic data may also be specified (see Precision in Chapter C1). String data must be given one of the attributes CHARACTER(length) or BIT(length), where length is an integer between 1 and 256, and may be given the attribute VARYING. For the declaration of structures, see Structures in Chapter C1.

DO ... END - This pair of keywords is used for two purposes in PL/I. The first is to bracket a group of statements or compound statements to form a compound statement. For example

```
DO;
 statement-1;
 statement-2;
 ...
 statement-n;
 END;
```

is a compound statement that can appear as a then or else clause, or anywhere that a single statement can appear. DO ... END is also used to specify a program loop. for example, the set of statements

```
DO I = 1 TO N BY K WHILE (A > B);
  list of statements
  END;
```

causes the list of statements to be executed for a sequence of values of I. In this example, the sequence of values is 1, 1+K, 1+2*K, ... until I exceeds N (is less than N if K is negative) and as long as A is greater than B. Formally, in the statements

```
DO I = exp1 TO exp2 BY exp3 WHILE(cond);
   ...
   END;
```

the values of exp1, exp2, and exp3 are evaluated before the loop is executed for the first time. I is assigned the value of exp1. If this is no larger than the value of exp2 (no less than if exp3 is negative), the logical value inside the WHILE clause is evaluated. If this is true the loop is executed for the first time, otherwise it is terminated. If it is not terminated, I is incremented by the original value of exp3 and the process is repeated. Note that the values of exp1, exp2 and exp3 are not changed even if variables appearing in them are changed inside the loop. The WHILE(cond) may be absent, or the counting specification "I = exp1 ... BY exp3" may be absent. In the latter case, the loop is executed as long as the logical value in the WHILE clause is true. In the former case, the counting specification controls the loop execution. The counting specification can consist of several simple specifications, for example,

```
DO I = 1 TO 10 BY 2, 15, 20 TO 40 BY 4;
```

This causes the loop to be executed with I taking the values 1, 3, 5, 7, 9, 15, 20, 24, 28, 32, 36, and 40 in turn. The "BY exp3" can be omitted, in which case the increment is one. The BY and TO clauses may have their positions interchanged. The loop controlled variable is not restricted to integer values; the values it can take depend on its declaration. For example,

```
DO A = 1.3 TO 3.9 BY 1.3
```

executes a loop with A equal to 1.3, 2.6, and 3.9--provided that A has been appropriately declared.

END - This statement terminates procedures started with the PROCEDURE statement, blocks started with the BEGIN statement, and compound statements or loops started with the DO statement. If a label appears after the END, it must be the same as the label appearing in front of the statement begining the structure.

ENTRY - See PROCEDURE.

FLOW A PL/C statement. Turns the FLOW condition on.

GET - The GET statement is used for reading character data and converting it into internal form. The three forms of the GET statement are:

```
GET LIST (list);
GET DATA;
GET EDIT (list) (format);
```

where list is a list of variables to be input and format is a description of the format to be used. The list of variables can include simple variables, arrays (in which case each element of the array is input in row order), or structures (in which case the elements are input in order of definition). The option SKIP(exp) may appear before or after the the keywords LIST, DATA, or EDIT. The expression exp is evaluated, and its integer value is used to SKIP to the begining of the appropriate line. A value of 1 or less causes input to start at the begining of the next line, a value of 2 advances to the beginning of the line after next, and so on.

GET LIST reads data in a free format. Data items must be separated by a comma and/or one or more blanks.
GET DATA reads data in the form name=value, name=value, ..., name=value; where each name is a variable name known to the GET statement causing the input, and each value is a constant.
GET EDIT reads the data according to the format specified in format. Format descriptors are described in Chapters <u>P6</u> and <u>P9</u>. The format descriptors are:

A - Character String
B - Bit String
C - Complex
E - Floating Point
F - Fixed Point
X - Space

The keyword GET may be followed by one of the options .
FILE(filename)
STRING(string-variable name) If neither is specified, the file SYSPRINT is assumed. If FILE is specified, the user must define the file named. This is not covered in this manual as it is system dependent. If STRING is specified, string-variable name must be the name of a character string known to the GET statement. The character string is used to provide a string of characters as input to the GET statement.

GO TO - is followed by a label. The label must be defined within a block or procedure containing the GO TO. It causes a immediate branch to the statement labelled. It should be used used sparingly to handle special loop exits.

IF ... THEN ... ELSE - is the basic selection statement in PL/I. Its general form is

```
IF logical expression
   THEN statement;
   ELSE statement;
```

The logical expression is evaluated. If it is true, the statement following the THEN is executed, otherwise the statement following the ELSE is executed. (Actually, the logical expression is a bit string. If any of the bits in the string is a one, the THEN is executed.) Although PL/I allows the ELSE and its statement to be omitted, it is not recommended. If there is no else clause, use the null statement represented by a semicolon. Either of the statements may be replaced by a compound statement or block. Note that in PL/C the logical expression must yield a bit string. In PL/I, any expression can be used. It will be converted to a bit string. Do not use such options, even if you are not using PL/C!

NOCHECK A PL/C statement. It turns off the CHECK condition.

ON - The ON statement takes one of the forms

```
ON condition SYSTEM
ON condition On-unit
```

where condition is one of a number of conditions that can be detected by the system. Optionally, the condition can be followed by the keyword SNAP which causes a listing of the active blocks to be generated when the condition occurs. The conditions discussed in this manual include ENDFILE, OVERFLOW, UNDERFLOW, ZERODIVIDE, FIXEDOVERFLOW, and SUBSCRIPTRANGE. There are many others beyond the scope of this manual. When an ON statement is executed it tells the system what to do when the named condition arises; it does not initiate the action directly. If the first form is the last ON executed for the named condition, the standard system action is taken when the condition arises. (For example, ENDFILE causes termination of the program.) If the second form is the last ON statement to be executed for the condition, the On-unit is executed. This should normally be a single assignment or GO TO statement, although a block is allowed. It should not be labelled. It is best to restrict the use of this statement to loop exits for end-of-file conditions, and to special debugging use as discussed in Chapter P5. The active ON conditions are associated with blocks and procedures; that is, if an ON statement is executed inside a procedure or block, exit from that procedure or block causes the last ON statement executed in a containing procedure or block to be the controlling one again.

If SNAP is specified, an indication of where the erroneous condition occurred is printed.

PROCEDURE ... END - These statements bracket a procedure definition. The basic form of a procedure is:

```
name: PROCEDURE (parameter list) options;
   declarations
      body of procedure
   END name;
```

where name is the procedure name (which may appear after the END if desired). The parameter list is a list of variable names separated by commas, and the options are additional specifications. In the case of the main procedure (for which the parameter list and its surrounding parentheses are absent, the options must be OPTIONS(MAIN). In the case of a function, the options must include RETURNS(type) where type is the data type of the result. The other options is the keyword RECURSIVE.

A procedeure should also be declared in any section of code that uses it in the form

DECLARE name ENTRY (parameter type list) RETURNS(type);

where parameter type list is a list of types of parameters to be passed, and the optional part RETURNS(type) specifies the type of result in the case of a function.

If a parameter is an array, it should be declared inside the procedure using * as the dimension--for example, a two-dimensional array is declared as X(*,*). A procedure may be given multiple entry points by use of the ENTRY statement. (This should only be done sparingly, as it does not lead to the best program structure.)

PUT - is the output statement for conversion between internal form and characters. It can take the four forms

```
PUT vertical option;
PUT LIST (expression list) vertical option;
PUT DATA (variable list) vertical option;
PUT EDIT (expression list) (format) vertical option;
```

where vertical option is a specification of vertical page movement. It is optional, except in the first case, and can include either PAGE, PAGE,LINE(exp), LINE(exp), or SKIP(exp) which cause the line to be output to start at the beginning of an appropriate new line (see Chapter P6 for details). The vertical option may also appear after the the keyword PUT. PUT LIST prints the values of the expressions listed. PUT DATA prints the values of the variables along with the variable names. It is particularly useful for diagnostic printing. PUT EDIT allows the user to specify the format precisely. (See Chapter P6 for details.) The keyword PUT may be followed by one of the options
FILE(filename)
STRING(string-variable name) If neither is specified, the file SYSIN is assumed. If FILE is specified, the user must define the file named. This is not covered in this manual as it is system dependent. If STRING is specified, string-variable name must be the name of a character string known to the PUT statement. The character string is assigned the output generated by the PUT statement. If STRING is specified, the PAGE and LINE options may not be used.

In PL/C, the statements

```
PUT ALL
PUT ARRAY
```

can be used to cause a listing of all simple variables, or all variables currently active.

RETURN - returns control from a subprocedure to a calling procedure. If the subprocedure is a function, the keyword RETURN should be followed with the value of the function in parentheses, for example, RETURN(3.4E2*A - B);. The expression is evaluated, converted to the type specified in the procedure statement, and returned as the value of the function.

Structure Assignment - If an assignment statement uses the name of a structure or substructure as one of the operands, the assignment statement is executed for each simple variable in the structure. All other operands in the expression must either be simple variables, or structures with exactly the same form. The left-hand side must be a structure of the same form. For example, if we have declared the structure Z by

```
DCL 1 Z(9), 2 (P,Q,R) FLOAT DEC;
```

the statement

```
Z(1) = Z(2) + Z(3);
```

is equivalent to the three statements

```
Z(1).P = Z(2).P + Z(3).P;
Z(1).Q = Z(2).Q + Z(3).Q;
Z(1).R = Z(2).R + Z(3).R;
```

C3 PL/I AND PL/C BUILT-IN FUNCTIONS

This chapter gives a list of some of the PL/I and PL/C functions. Unless specified otherwise, all work in PL/C and PL/I.

Arithmetic Built-in Functions

The functions expect arithmetic values as arguments, and return arithmetic values of the same type as results unless indicated otherwise. Most of these functions will accept arrays as arguments, in which case they return arrays of the same size as results. For example, the ABS of a ten-element array is a ten-element array whose entries are the absolute values of the ten entries of the original array.

ABS(P)	Absolute value of P
CEIL(P)	The smallest integer at least as large as P. P may not be COMPLEX. The type of CEIL is the type of P; that is, CEIL(4.7E0) is 5.0E0.
COMPLEX(P,Q)	The complex number P + Q*1I. P and Q must be REAL.
CONJG(P)	The complex conjugate of the COMPLEX argument P.
FIXED(P)	The FIXED form of P.
FLOAT(P)	The FLOAT form of P.
FLOOR(P)	The largest integer not exceeding P. P must not be COMPLEX. See the comment on CEIL regarding data types.
IMAG(P)	The imaginary part of COMPLEX P.
MAX(P1, P2, ..., Pn)	The maximum value of P1 through Pn. The type is the "highest" type of the arguments. (E.g. FLOAT is higher than FIXED.) The arguments must be REAL.
MIN(P1, P2, ..., Pn)	The minimum value of P1 through Pn. The type is the "highest" type of the arguments. (E.g. FLOAT is higher than FIXED.) The arguments must be REAL.
MOD(P,Q)	The remainder when P is divided by Q an integral number of times. The remainder lies between 0 and ABS(Q). The arguments must not be COMPLEX.
REAL(P)	The real part of the complex argument P.
ROUND(P,N)	The FIXED number P is rounded at the Nth digit after the point. If N is zero, P is rounded to an integer, if N is negative, it is rounded in the N+1th digit to the right of the point. Remember that the effect of anything but N = 0 depends on the base, whether decimal or binary.
SIGN(P)	The result is a FIXED BINARY value equal to -1, 0, 1 as the argument P is negative, zero, or positive. P must not be complex.
TRUNC(P)	The integer furthest from zero that is not further from zero than P. P must not be complex.

C3 PL/I AND PL/C BUILT-IN FUNCTIONS

Mathematical Built-in Functions

Arguments to these functions are automatically converted to floating point if they are not already in that form. The argument may be real or complex, and the result will have the same form unless stated otherwise. Arrays may be passed as arguments except where noted.

ATAN(X)	The arctangent of X.
ATAN(X,Y)	The arctangent of X/Y in radians. Both arguments must be real.
ATAND(X,Y)	The arctangent of X/Y in degrees. X and Y must be real.
ATANH(X)	The hyperbolic arctangent of X. X must be real and a least 1.
COS(X)	Cosine of X radians.
COSD(X)	Cosine of X degrees.
COSH(X)	The hyperbolic cosine of X.
EXP(X)	e**X where e is the base of the natural logarithm.
LOG(X)	The natural logarithm of X. If X is real, it must be greater than 0, if complex, it may not be zero.
LOG10(X)	The base 10 logarithm of X. X must be real and positive.
LOG2(X)	The base 2 logarithm of X. X must be real and positive.
RAND(X)	PL/C only. Generates a sequence of pseudo random numbers. Should normally be used in form X = RAND(X); where X is FLOAT REAL and the initial value of X should be between zero and one.
SIN(X)	The sine of X radians.
SIND(X)	The sine of X degrees.
SINH(X)	The hyperbolic sine of X.
SQRT(X)	The square root of X. If X is real, it must be non-negative.
TAN(X)	The tangent of X radians.
TAND(X)	The tangent of X degrees.
TANH(X)	The hyperbolic tangent of X.

String Handling Built-in Functions

The functions operate on and/or return strings. They can also operate on array arguments and return array results unless noted otherwise.

HIGH(N)	A character string of length N consisting of the highest characters in the collating sequence. That is, HIGH(256) is guaranteed to be no less than any permissible PL/I character string. N must be a FIXED DECIMAL constant.

C3 PL/I AND PL/C BUILT-IN FUNCTIONS

INDEX(S,P)	The arguments can be BIT or CHARACTER strings. The result is a FIXED BINARY integer giving the index of the first character in S where the substring P occurs, or zero if it doesn't appear.
LENGTH(S)	The length of the BIT or CHARACTER string S. The result is FIXED BINARY.
LOW(N)	A character string of length N containing the lowest character in the collating sequence. N must be a decimal integer constant.
REPEAT(S,N)	A string consisting of N repeats of the string S. N must be a decimal integer constant.
STRING(X)	X must be a variable, structure or array consisting only of character strings. The result is the concatenation of all these strings.
SUBSTR(S,N1,N2)	The substring of string S, starting at the N1th character and continuing for N2 characters. N2 and its preceding comma can be omitted, in which case the substring continues to the end of S.
VERIFY(S,P)	S and P and strings. The result is the index of the first character cr bit in S which is not in P. P is simply a set of characters, all of which are checked against each character of S. If every character (or bit) in S is in P, the result is zero

__Array Built-in Functions__

These functions accept arrays as arguments, and return scalars.

ALL(X)	X must be an array of bit strings. The result is the string obtained by and-ing them all together--that is, bit i in the result is a one only if all bits in the array in bit position i are ones.
ANY(X)	Similar to ALL, but an "or" is performed, so the result is a one in position i if any of the strings in X have a one in position i.
DIM(X,N)	The number of entries in the Nth dimension of the array X, that is, the high bound minus the low bound plus 1 for that dimension.
HBOUND(X,N)	The high bound of the Nth dimension of X.
LBOUND(X,N)	The low bound of the Nth dimension of X.
PROD(X)	The product of all of the elements in array X.
SUM(X)	The sum of all of the elements in array X.

__Other Built-in Functions__

DATE	A character string of length 6 giving the date. Two characters are provided for year, month, and day. Thus, Feb. 6, 1979 is represented as 790206.
TIME	A nine character string giving the time of day in the form hours (two characters), minutes (two characters), seconds (two characters), and milli-seconds (three characters). Thus, 5.33 p.m. plus several seconds might appear as 173315310.

C4 DIFFERENCES BETWEEN PL/C AND PL/I

Since PL/C is designed to make debugging easy, it differs from PL/I by having a few additional statements and different default conditions. PL/C also includes a number of options that can be specified on the $PLC card that are helpful for debugging. In addition, some PL/I statements are not implemented in PL/C in order to keep the compiler to a manageable size. This chapter summarizes the principal differences between the two languages and the additions in PL/C.

Additional Features in PL/C

The main additional features in PL/C are the statements

```
         FLOW
         NOFLOW
         CHECK
and      NOCHECK
```

which are described in Chapter P5. Use of these will make a program incompatible with PL/I. However, this can be avoided by using the PL/C pseudo-comment facility. This is a line that looks exactly like a comment to PL/I, but the first character inside the comment must be a digit 1 through 7 or a colon. If, on the $PL/C card, the option CMNTS(list) is specified, all comments with a colon or one of the digits in the list as their first character will have the comment quotes and the first character replaced by blanks. For example, if we have the line

```
/*2 FLOW; CHECK;  */
```

in our program, this will be seen by PL/I as a comment. However, if the $PLC line includes the option CMNTS(2,3), for example, the line will be converted to the line

```
    FLOW; CHECK;
```

before being processed by the PL/C compiler. This enables us to write programs that can be run under either PL/C or PL/I.

PL/C is more forgiving of many minor errors, and will frequently give warnings about language usage that is not acceptable to PL/I. As a general rule, it is wise to code in such a way that no such warnings are generated.

Options on the $PLC card

A number of options can be specified on the $PLC card. These include those shown below. The form of the PLC card is

```
$PLC option-1 option-2 ... option-n
```

where each option is separated from the next by spaces and/or a comma. The options may be abbreviated to the one- or two-letter form indicated following the full form in brackets, and may be preceded by NO to turn the option off. For example,

```
$PLC A, NODE CMNTS(1)
```

causes an attribute listing, prevents a dump on error, and converts comments whose first character is : or 1 to statements.

ATR [A] Causes a listing of the attributes of each identifier to be printed. Normally off.

BNDRY [B] Strings and comments are limited to a single card. Normally on.

CMNTS [C] or CMNTS(i1, i2, ...). Comments with : in first position are converted to statements by removing the comment quotes. If parameters are given, comments with digits 1 through 7 as their first character are also converted if the digit is listed as a parameter. Normally off.

DUMP [D] or DUMP(d1, d2, ...). Produces a dump at termination. The parameters indicate what will be dumped. Parameters can include
- BLOCKS [B] All blocks active at termination
- SCALARS [S] Final values of all scalars at termination
- ARRAYS [A] Final values of all arrays at termination
- FLOW [F] List of last 18 transfers of control
- LABELS [L] List of labels used with the number of times corresponding statement executed
- ENTRIES [E] List of entry names with frequency of calling
- REPORT [R] Statistics on run time, core usage, etc.
- UNREAD [U] List of first five unread data lines
- Integer depth. An integer parameter giving a limit on the number of active blocks dumped in the B, S and A options. Zero means unlimited

If no parameters are given, all but ARRAY are assumed with unlimited depth. DUMP is normally off.

DUMPE [DE] or DUMPE(d1, d2, ...). This produces a dump only if an error occurs during execution. Normally on with the same defaults as DUMP. The parameters are the same as for DUMP.

DUMPT [DT] or DUMPT(d1, d2, ...). As for DUMPE, but only if an error terminates execution. Normally on.

SORMGIN=(f,e) [SM] sets source line margins so that a PL/C statement is read from columns f to e inclusive. Default is 2 to 72.

SOURCE [S] prints a listing of the source program. Normally on.

XREF [X] list the cross references, that is all uses of each identifier. Normally off.

C4.1 PL/C Restrictions

A number of PL/I attributes and statements are not included in PL/C. The only item discussed in this manual that is not a part of PL/C is the pointer attribute. The other differences are listed below.

Reserved Words - Some of the keywords are reserved in PL/C but not PL/I. A list of keywords appears in Chapter C1 with an indication of those that are reserved. These must not be used as identifiers.

PL/I provides for additional automatic conversion between data types, for example, between CHARACTER and numeric. It is not a good idea to use these features of PL/I because they are both inefficient and likely to hide coding errors.

C4.1 PL/C Restrictions

The defaults on some conditions are different in PL/C. These are such that PL/C is more likely to print error messages than PL/I. For example, SUBSCRIPTRANGE is normally on in PL/C and off in PL/I. (See Chapter P5.)

Comments in PL/C are restricted to a single card unless an option is specified on the $PLC line. (The option is NOBNDRY.)

PL/C does all of its floating-point arithmetic in double precision (on the IBM 370) whereas PL/I uses single precision unless the specified precision exceeds 7 decimal digits or 21 binary digits.

The size of program allowed (which is a complicated combination of the amount of nesting of procedures, blocks, DO groups, IF statements, and numbers of identifiers) is generally smaller in PL/C. This will not affect the average size program.

Some PL/I and PL/C Reference Material

IBM OS PL/I Checkout and Optimizing Compilers Language Reference Manual, form GC33-00904, file # S360/370-29.

User's Guide to PL/C, The Cornell Compiler for PL/I, Release 7, June 1974, Cornell University Department of Computer Science.

An Introduction to Programming: A Structured Approach Using PL/I and PL/C-7, Conway, R., and Gries, D., Second Edition, Winthrop Publishers, Cambridge, Mass. 1975

INDEX